1. Fire's origin
2. Q.T.
3. Pumpkin found
4. Disney
5. Marduk
6. Parkwood Apts.
7. Timothy
8. Dudley
9. Max Smith
10. Gus

11. Bud & Princess
12. Mr. Fox
13. Chad
14. Charmian
15. Mamalucci
16. Katrina
17. Pumpkin's home
18. Max Hofmann
19. D. J.

OPERATION PET RESCUE

Animal Survivors of the Oakland, California, Firestorm

Gregory N. Zompolis

J. N. TOWNSEND PUBLISHING
EXETER, NEW HAMPSHIRE
1994

Jacket photo by Karol Cummins.

Printed in the United States by BookCrafters.

Published by
J. N. Townsend Publishing
12 Greenleaf Drive
Exeter, New Hampshire 03833
(603) 778-9883

First Printing.

Library of Congress Cataloging-in-Publication Data
Zompolis, Gregory N., 1952-
    Operation pet rescue : animal survivors of the Oakland, Cali-
fornia, firestorm / Gregory N. Zompolis.
    p. cm.
    ISBN 1-880158-04-3
    1. Cats--California--Oakland--anecdotes. 2. Cats--California--
Berkeley--Anecdotes. 3. Dogs--California--Oakland--Anecdotes. 4.
Dogs--Berkeley--Anecdotes. 5 Fires--California--Oakland. 6. Fires-
-California--Berkeley. 7 Wildfires--California--Oakland. 8. Wildfires-
-California--Berkeley. 9 Animal rescue--California--Oakland. 10.
Animal rescue--California--Berkeley. I. Title. II. Title: Pet rescue.
    SF442.63.U6Z66   1994
    636.8'09747'65--dc20   94-19616
                                                CIP

Contents

Foreword

I wish that I had never had the chance to write this book. That is not to say that I am not grateful it is being published, but I wish that the firestorm had never occurred and that this story would never have to be told. The pain and suffering, physical as well as emotional, of the animals and humans portrayed here are not easy to write about. However, the courageous tales I have recounted here deserve to be shared with those who love animals.

From the beginning of my work with the Firestorm Pet Rescue operation I was awarded the opportunity of meeting so many wonderful people and participating in the happy reunions with their pets, many of whom survived the fire against all odds. This book is about their survival and the indomitable spirit of love.

I have known the unwavering love of pets throughout my life. My first dog, Jiggs, a Maltese, was my faithful companion from the time he was a week old until he died almost eighteen years later. Zip, a tiny tabby kitten arrived at two o'clock one summer morning and stayed for fifteen years. Semper, a Doberman and shepherd mix, shared thirteen and a half years with me, enriching each one with his loving ways and gentle manners. Boots I only knew for a few months before he succumbed but he was one of the most affectionate cats on earth. Kitkit, presently with me, was a pregnant teenager when I found her who gave birth to five kittens under my bed in 1988. Only one was adopted and I see him frequently where he lives near my mother's home. The four kittens I kept—Harold, mehitabel, Apollo and Shy—have been the joy of my life and indisputable members of my family. Shy passed away unexpectedly in August 1993, while I was writing this book. In June 1992, Sam, an unclaimed cat from the firestorm, came to share our home.

I have known the love and affection of wonderful animals, and I have experienced the acute pain of losing them, yet I have not known the desperation that the survivors of the Oakland/Berkeley firestorm experienced in not knowing what happened to their own companions.

During the course of writing this book, my life was disrupted twice by nearby fires and I prepared to evacuate. The first one was only moments after beginning the book. I must have been on the third paragraph. Later, toward the end, a home only about one hundred and fifty feet from mine caught on fire. We were separated by a wall of eucalyptus and pine trees, excellent fuel for windswept embers. Fortunately, these fires were contained, but all the lessons which I have learned from the Oakland/Berkeley fire swarmed through my head. I received a first hand lesson in what so many people before me had experienced on that fateful day: it can happen to anyone.

It has been a rewarding time helping to find these pets and to reunite them with their people. I met so many wonderful people and animals during the course of this rescue. I am grateful to those who took the time from their busy lives to share their stories with me. A significant portion of this book's proceeds will go directly to animal causes, many of which are named in the text.

My only regret is that we could not find them all.

Greg Zompolis
October 20, 1993

This book is dedicated to all of those who did not come back:

Cody	Hannibal	Ketzel	Moqui
Lucifer	Sammy	Annapurna	Star
Emma	Jasmine	Romeo	Comeback
Sandy	Gretal	Cuddles	Esmeralda
Sasha	Dirac	Alex	Freeway
Nadia	Kika	Mikos	Billy
Marilyn	Tom	Willie	Babe
Persephony	Kitty	Gus	Mad Max
Kitty	Thea	Coco	Emma
Hugo	Henry	Action	Nemo
Tosha	Hay	Oliver	Jinx
Natasha	Niko	Capt. Wow	Sheena
Halstead	Zucchini	Eddie	Kaos
One Eye	Oreo	Fluffy	Vincent
Tinker	Mama Kitty	Bip	Rover
Inky	Jeepster	Malcolm	Killer
Tiger	Busha	Muslei	Snowball
Ralph	Tigre	Skippy	Wellington
Angel	Zuma	Trump	Zucchini
Jake	Boots	Sister	Zippy
Piggy	Brandy	Sebastian	J.J.
Midnight	Susanna	Leslie	Samantha
Fluffy	Misty	Bazooka	Snaggles
Rio	Baby Doe	Scurvy	Yardley
Teddy	Tom	Callie	Casper
Riki	Ralph	Nina	Footon
Rupert	Felini	Austin	Chester
Spooky	Barney	Al	Disney
Toughy	Scooby	Halstead	Fudge

Kitty	Patches	Stella	Chicago
Tigger	Petina	Squeak	Sophie
Tiffany	Sassi	Margaret Rose	Baby
Marlin	Moses	Max	Snale
Bunny	Pinky	Maggie	Panda
Bonni	Bob	Shadow	Thelma
Tiger	Miss Friendly	Dona	Pussums
Nephrititi	Tsugimas	Martha	Fefe
Suki	Sherbert	Shadow	Le Pew
Emily	Keiko	Mitzi	Gordie
Samantha	Carmel	Ritz	Bashful
Ne	Brutus	Kringle	Ivan
Tyler	Plunkett	Purr-Tiger	Haley
Nimby	Weber	Nana	Rocky
Fanny	Snix	Goldie	Jeremiah
Almond	Felix	Pretty Kitty	Sammy
Casey	Tashi	Stretch	Pickens
Dutchess	Alice	Puss	Muffin
Winston	Thorn	Casey	Busby
Sasha	Soli	Ruff	Tuffy
Hooker	Arthur	Mark	Jekyll
Chester	Sam	Baby Kitty	L.C.
Bori	Rocky	Topaz	Harry
Cougar	Jake	Lucky	Murphy
Newt	Tiga	Ummer	Oboe
Pumpkin	Sammy	Teeny	Marty
Bubba	Tyrone	Moosey	Maggie
Jezebel	Gretchen	Kriga	Sylvester
Max	Pookie	Fuzz Face	Blackie
Lily	Norman	Molly	Sam
C.W.	Basin	Samantha	Daphne
Mertle	Elwood	Toshi	Ceily
Mrs. Beasley	Caitlin	Misha	Andy
Douka	Dexter	Speckles	Mittens
Meyer	Chad	Silver	Alphie
Louie	Tiger	Samantha	Minnie
Malone	Little Princess	Serena	Punky Lunk
Toshiro	Shabagel	Alosia	Dimples
Scooter	Emily	Luke	Gumby
Crazy Legs	Coco	Pauline	Cocoa

Dude	Felix	Lobos	Rachel
Gregory	Shadow	Agnes	Ruggles
Tikal	Midnight	Cleo	Marvel
Abercrombie	Tardo	Haily	Jinx
Butch	Phoenix	Bacall	Missie
Lydia	Nikki	Erica	Pewter
Tiger	Muffin	Friskie	Putchy
Bart	Al	Rover	Mojo
Korky	Fluffy	Sweetpea	Star
Princess	Little Sweet	Felix	Spedzi
Alex	heart	Lionel	Bibi
Domino	Scooter	Rocky	Hop
Cougar	Bichou	Sam	Sing
John	Worm	Allie	Shaver
Topoly	Lady	Angus	Lucy
Spot	Jeffrey	Penny	Hugo
Frodo	Khyam	Snickers	Korky
Sundae	Messina	Shadrack	Prudence
Paws	Sammy	Freddie	Fu Bear
Johnathan	Bebe	Sammy	Guiness
Zero	Snorkie	Kitty	Tennessee
Sushi	Kaiko	Sweetie	Tammy
Ichabod	Kisha	Taffy	Erno
Natasha	Bounder	Charlie	Ali
Chelsea	Zucchini	Ms. Shoo	Max
Muffy	Howie	Kitty	Hobo
Squeaky	Cleo	Dood	Lucas
Tai	Bombay	Pooky	Affa
Isaak	Gemini	Smokey	Jake
Renee	Stripe	Tiger	Kitty
Peppers	Tiny	Doug	Rusty
Toby	Junior	Patches	Hans
Maywood	Guark	Jasper	Fezzy
Chicita	Snowy	Tiffany	Wig
Tasha	Puss	Momcat	Beau
Sergio	Abagail	Odie	Oscar
Max	Amelia	Spike	Mookie
Spooky	Why	Caramel	Polo
Oscar	Bogie	Ethel	Inu
Louie	Sherman	Tiggie	Happy

Zeuse	Bo	Kona	Fluff
Durga	Max	Snickers	Buddy
Sparky	Schatzi	Thomasina	Hoby
Sophie	Juan	T.J.	Tom
Max	Shandee	Clovey	Shelby
Ping	Kitty	Suzie	Frisky
Alex	Misty	Reddie	Bernie
Elwood	Sheba	Chiba	Tecate
Skipper	Abby	Lucky	Tweedie
Orbit	Fred	Tipsy	Brandy
Woe Woe	Teg	Blue	Gretta
Huckleberry	Henrietta	Casey	Gus
Ella	Maggie	Falkland	Junior
Nicky	Smokey	Koko	Honey
Sunshine	Sparky	Herbert	Theodore
Silver	Missy	Henry	Teddy
Jake	Sampson	Lucky	Bigfoot
Mindy	Rachel	Tyler	Kate

In memory of my mother, Muriel A. Zompolis (1923–1994), who instilled the love of all animals in me.

Part One:
THE FIRESTORM

Saturday, October 19, 1991

$\mathbf{F}$ew people living in the heavily forested hillsides behind Berkeley and Oakland, California, ever knew about the routine brush fire that occurred about 2:00 p.m. on Saturday, October 19, 1991. Those who did know about it paid scant attention to it. It quickly and quietly engulfed six acres in the Hiller Highlands area and was put out with speed and accuracy by the local fire crews according to regulations. It was normal this time of year to have such brush fires, and the extinguishing of the small fire was promptly attended to and forgotten by the fire department. They left their hoses nearby, unattached to any water sources and went on about other business. Other fires were occurring away from the hill area that needed their attention.

The six years of drought had left the hillsides all over northern California extremely dry. The previous winter's rainfall had been minimal, and the spring grasses rapidly turned from a fresh green to a crispy golden brown. The trees became drier as well, especially the non-native eucalyptus, which had been profusely planted all around the state decades ago as a source for lumber, but had proved unsatisfactory when the first ones had been felled, leaving the balance as landscaping. Their soft wood and shallow root system are a constant plague to homeowners. Quick to grow in the temperate California climate eucalypti provide shade and a unique scent that permeates the entire area.

The weather had been very hot, over ninety degrees, but that was not unusual for mid-October. Summer had imperceptibly blended into Indian summer in the northern half of the "Golden State."

The winds increased, sweeping down through the canyons, bringing a welcoming breeze to the area. As the afternoon of October 19 proceeded, the residents of the area went on about their weekend business. Many were away for the weekend, taking advantage of the weather. Many were abroad on business

The canyons and hills behind Oakland and Berkeley are densely populated, but the homes are secluded, cushioned by an immense amount of foliage. Many of the homes have spectacular views of San Francisco. It is a short drive across the Bay Bridge or a short ride on B.A.R.T. (Bay Area Rapid Transit) on sleek silver trains through a tunnel under San Francisco Bay to reach the City.

The homes are an eclectic mixture of architecture, from shingled Craftsman bungalows of the early part of the century designed by local architects who had achieved national fame, such as Bernard Maybeck, to stunning contemporary cubist structures that cling to the hillsides. Because of the mountainous terrain, many homes were built on extremely steep slopes. It is an affluent area where the residents enjoy the finer things in life. The University of California at Berkeley nudges its way towards the foot-hills, and the landmark Claremont Hotel stands guard as a dazzling white dowager, visible from all the way across the Bay.

Oakland residents have traditionally suffered from the elitist attitudes of their neightbors in San Francisco, although it recently ranked as one of America's most desir-able cities in a national contest. As far back as 1906, people refused to live in Oakland even though they had lost their homes in the fire that destroyed San Francisco after the earthquake that year. However, those who know Oakland realize that they live in a lovely city and defend it fiercely, citing its advantages, and refusing to live elsewhere. The area of the hills is like a world unto itself. Artists, writers, and poets inhabit the wooded setting along with the doc-tors, lawyers, and accountants. It seems so removed from the flatlands of the city. But it was not without problems. In 1901, a fire in the Berkeley Hills destroyed the original Claremont Hotel structure. Twenty-two years later, on September 17, 1923, 584 homes were lost in a 72-block area to a wildfire. The scenario was repeated again on Sep-tember 22, 1970 when a brush fire destroyed 37 homes in the Buckingham Boulevard/Marlborough Terrace area and damaged several others.

Oakland again suffered a terrible shock on October 17, 1989 when the Loma Prieta Earthquake collapsed free-way ramps onto each other like pancakes at the Cypress Street structure, resulting in numerous deaths. Many cars were crushed to just a few inches in height. The world watched as the living and dead were extricated over the next four days.

3

Barely two years after that tragic event, Oakland and Berkeley had regained a semblance of normal life, but it would last only a few more hours.

Saturday, October 19, 1991

Caryn Gottlieb had an overwhelming sense that something terrible was going to happen to her cat, Zeb. She had never thought of herself as psychic, but the feeling of dread would not leave her this Saturday afternoon. She repeatedly held him and told him that everything was going to be all right. She knew that he was going to experience something awful, but the same intuitive sense told her that the outcome was going to be a good one for him.

At her townhouse in Hiller Highlands, Terri Hensley swept a fine powder of ash from her entry deck. She had not seen a fire nor smelled one, but here was the evidence that one had occurred. She thought that maybe it was from a controlled burn to get rid of brush. She gave no more thought to it as she cleaned it up and put the broom away in the garage. She had just moved into the townhouse with her new husband, Rod, and a daughter from her previous marriage, Kelli Smith. When she went inside, she remembers having to close the windows because the wind was whipping the drapes about. She hated to do it because it was such a warm day, but she feared having a lamp or two knocked over. Max, Kelli's cat, sat on the deck near the living room, oblivious to the panoramic view, but jumping slightly every time a gust of wind made something else in the house make a noise.

Evening came, and an apricot and lemon sunset drenched the sky behind San Francisco before being swallowed by the Pacific Ocean. The residents of the hills settled into a Saturday night routine, many taking advantage of the fine cafés and restaurants nearby. The gelaterias on College Avenue were packed with people enjoying the sweet Italian ices during the warm evening. The theaters enjoyed a brisk business, most of them showing the more obscure, artistic films, appreciated by the local University crowd.

On Contra Costa Road, Nancy Rogers became worried as the night sky darkened. Her calico cat, Princess, had not come inside. The hours went by and Nancy checked and rechecked for Princess. She knew that there must be a serious reason for Princess not to show up. Nancy dreaded making a trip to the pound and wondered if her adult son, Bill, who was staying with her, would have time after his workout at the local gym tomorrow morning to accompany her. As she drifted off to sleep, Nancy waited for the familiar "thump" as Princess jumped on her dresser and then over to her bed, but it never came.

Sunday, October 20, 1991 —
5 a.m. to 10:58 p.m.

Bob Adamson was awakened by the wind shortly after five o'clock. It was unnatural for northern California to have such winds. These were like the desert winds, or Santa Anas, that blew hot across Los Angeles. The morning looked sunny and the day would probably be as hot as it had been the day before.

Norma Armon sat at her computer in her home office on Swainland Drive. The morning was perfect—quiet and not too warm yet. Norma felt she was at peak efficiency, getting work done for her business translation service before breakfast. In a nearby chair, her ten-year-old Abyssinian-mix cat, Charmian, watched Norma as her fingers flew over the keyboard. Norma played their favorite music, Brahms, softly in the background.

Life unraveled slowly for the other residents of the hillsides that morning. They went to church, or sipped coffee while enjoying the morning paper. Stan Smith kissed his wife, Virginia, goodbye and stroked the ears of their dog, Dudley, as he left to meet their friends for a round of golf. Jimmy Reina and Elaine Gerber let their cats Mamalucci, Simi, and Mookie outdoors to explore around their yard while they took their ailing fourteen-year-old standard poodle, Lido, to the vet's. He had an electrolyte imbalance and had almost died the previous week, but had rallied and they were encouraged by his recovery. Nearby, a neighbor of Carol and Nick Martin slipped inside their house to feed their cat, Delta Joe, or "D.J." before going off to a brunch in San Francisco. D.J. , a wholly indoors cat, insisted on staying in their son Paul's room.

It had been twenty-four hours since Caryn Gottlieb's feeling of doom had hit her, and nothing had happened, so she tried to dismiss the feeling as she drove off across the Bay Bridge at about ten o'clock. She was certain that whatever the feeling had been was utter nonsense, yet, uncharacteristically, she gave her housemate the number of her friend's house where she could be reached "in case the house burns down or something."

In Hiller Highlands, Dorothy Sparks took her Papillion dog, Nellie, for her regular morning walk. Her new charge, Gus, a three-year-old orange cat, whom she had adopted at the request of a dying friend seven months earlier, accompanied them as he did every morning, zigzagging in front and behind them, exploring the bushes, and darting into Nellie's path as a "surprise."

Ron and Carol Hofmann began early preparations for their Hallowe'en party. Carol put up the decorations on the outside of the house, carefully placing the spooky witches and smiling pumpkins and stretching the ersatz spiderwebs in the corners of the porch. Pleased with her artistic endeavor, she fed the family's five cats, who ranged in age from Natasha, age fifteen, to the "baby" of the clan, Max, who at nine months of age was full of the exploration and wonder that marks a kitten's life. A leaf, a gust of wind, a sibling's twitching tail were all cause for intense scrutiny. As a Flamepoint Siamese, Max had the characteristic slenderness of the breed and the unique blue eyes, but his points were orange instead of brown or gray.

Terri Hensley left her Hiller Highlands townhouse to check in on the family business in Alameda, a small city on the bayfront, leaving her sixteen-year-old daughter, Kelli, asleep in her bedroom on the lowest level of the hillside townhouse. Her husband, Rod, was due to return from a business trip that afternoon, and Terri had planned to meet him at the airport after looking in on the business.

Miles away, in downtown Berkeley, Bill Rogers, Nancy Rogers' son, pumped away at the weights at Gold's Gym. His golden retreiver/lab mix, Bud, waited patiently in Bill's jeep.

Diana Ragen expected to have a peaceful Sunday in her home on upper Broadway Terrace. None of her three cats had been around this morning, but she did not pay much heed to this. With such beautiful weather, no one should have to stay indoors. She briefly saw a flash of one cat, although she could not identify which one it was as she slid past the deck. Pumpkin and Samantha were the youngest, while Sundae at nine years old, had belonged to Diana's late mother.

Everyone went about a normal Sunday routine, including the Oakland Fire Department and the California Department of Forestry. They met at the site of the six-acre brush fire that had occurred the previous afternoon on a routine follow-up check. Three hot spots were found, and from the top of the ridge, the Oakland Fire Department extinguished two of them. The other fire crew put out the third.

At 10:58 a.m., the fire department called in a first alarm when a light cloud of smoke appeared from the bottom of the hillside near Buckingham Boulevard. Tiny tongues of flame had somehow rekindled in the remaining, unburned dry grasses of the hillside. There was little cause for concern until the fire swept up the hill in a few seconds, gaining both momentum and volume.

10:58 a.m. to 11:27 a.m.

Margaret Power saw the first flash of flame leap up the hillside below her home on Marlborough Terrace. It had come from nowhere. Her sense of survival told her to get out of the house. She had lost her home in the fire of 1970, and knew better than to wait around. She would come back later after the fire was out. Margaret briefly looked for her cat, Mittens, as she went through her living room, but could not find him. She felt as if she were walking in slow motion. She wondered if she should try to take anything. "What does it matter?" she thought, and grabbed her car keys and purse. Outside, the air was rapidly filling with smoke. Neighbors all around were beginning to leave their homes as the flames came closer and closer. Margaret drove down the hill as the sound of sirens filled the smoky air.

Sybil Maguire, another resident of Marlborough Terrace, called 9-1-1 and reported the fire at the bottom of the hill behind her house. Moments later, emergency services called her back and she was told that it would be attended to immediately. Less than a minute later, the fire exploded. Then she knew that she and her husband, Steven, would have to evacuate as they had the previous day when the six acres were consumed. They had also lost their home in the 1970 fire and wasted no time in departing as the thickening smoke enveloped the hillside.

On Marlborough Terrace, history was repeating itself. Officially a Berkeley address, the street was within the Oakland city limit, causing confusion as to which fire department would respond. The fire had grown tremendously in just a few minutes, and was starting to burn the houses that had previously burned in 1970. The wind whipped the flames about. They encircled the pine and eucalyptus trees on the hillside, turning them into towering torches within seconds.

The fire department reached Marlborough Terrace as the houses were being overwhelmed. Juanita Simpson walked to the bottom of her driveway, which was blocked by a fire truck, and asked a firefighter to let her know if the situation became worse. Before she could reach her front door, another fireman called to her to "get your cats and GET OUT!" One of her cats, Oliver, was terminally ill with kidney disease. She had brought him home for their final days together, trying to keep him as comfortable as possible. Juanita had hoped that he would die peacefully in her arms and spare her having to make a decision to put him to sleep. She put Oliver in a cardboard cat carrier and placed another of her cats, Melvin, in a separate carrier, and left her home on foot. Her two other cats, Cassey and Trent, refused to come near her.

Outside on the street, the smoke had thickened considerably, making breathing difficult. Most residents had fled. The fire truck sirens could be heard mingled with the roar of the flames. It was getting difficult to see. Juanita found her neighbor, Margaret Power, coming up the road, having abandoned her car on the blocked street. It was then that a police car arrived. Officer Michael McArthur was on patrol on Marlborough Terrace. He said that although he ordered everyone he encountered to evacuate, almost all refused. People were going towards the fire, not away from it. Most wanted to see for themselves how bad the situation was. Officer McArthur found Margaret Powers and Juanita Simpson standing by the side of the road with two cat carriers. He ordered them into his squad car, but they told him that they wanted to see about their homes. Again, he ordered them into the car. They complied, each holding a carrier in her lap as Officer McArthur got on the radio.

Both sides of Marlborough Terrace were now ablaze. The fire was moving fast, and igniting treetops as it swooped down on the neighborhood. Officer McArthur descended the street and when he encountered the same blockage that Margaret had, he made what he describes as the "fastest three point turn in history" to go up Marlborough Terrace, in the direction of Grizzly Peak. Within seconds, he saw another woman at the curb, pulled over, and jumped out of his vehicle, ordering her to get into it. She looked at him and turned and ran back into her home, which had already caught fire. He knew there was not enough time to pursue her, and jumped back into his car. He could easily lose three human and two feline lives while attempting to force the woman into his vehicle. All that the occupants of the car could see was orange flame surrounding them. The roar of the fire as it bore down on them became deafening. Officer McArthur had no other choice but to drive into the flames. He feared he had waited seconds too long and that their fate was sealed. All around him the fire closed in, lashing against the black and white patrol car. It was impossible to see even an inch ahead as the thick black smoke billowed about them. Embers blew over the hood of the car. It could ignite at any moment. Over his radio, a motorcycle cop at the top of Grizzly Peak assured McArthur that there was clear air up at the peak and advised him to proceed up the street, not down it towards the city. McArthur did not know what lay ahead of them and, engulfed in smoke and fire, turned on his blue and red light bar and siren and shot forward into the inferno. He had to zigzag around abandoned fire trucks, obstacles he had not expected to find in his path. Suddenly they emerged out of the flames and into the light and clear air. Waiting to greet them was the relieved and smiling motorcycle cop.

The sixth alarm was called in at 11:27 a.m., but by then it was pointless. A swirling pillar of smoke arose above the hillside community, pulling in the strong winds of the morning to help fuel its destruction

11:27 a.m. to 12:15 p.m.

The fire raced along. It rolled over the canyon in which it had originated bearing down on Hiller Highlands. It headed for the Parkwood Apartments on Caldecott Lane, a complex of four hundred units that sat in the small valley between ridges. Before anyone knew it, it was spreading in too many directions to count. It leapt from treetop to treetop to roof. Many homes, clad in rustic shake roofs, caught fire immediately. People stayed behind to fight it with slender garden hoses. There was so little time to flee, let alone look for an elusive, frightened pet or to grab treasured possessions. No one had expected all this and it all happened so quickly. People stood in disbelief, waiting for an official word from authorities to evacuate. It never came in many instances, because the fire got there first.

The roads, narrow and twisting, many of them only able to accommodate one vehicle at a time, became quagmires. Forced to abandon their cars, residents ran down the hillsides. The abandoned automobiles created further obstacles for the crew trying to fight the conflagration. The cars exploded as the fire enveloped them, adding to the ferocious roar of the wall of flame. The winds had reached a speed of forty miles per hour. The humidity that day was at only ten percent, drastically low. The conditions were perfect for a firestorm, an event always dreaded by any fire department.

An epic battle against nature had begun. The call went out to neighboring communities for help. The fire grew exponentially and efforts to quench it were futile. A helicopter scooped water from Lake Temescal, but its relative thimblefuls were no match for the growing inferno. The fire swept around in multiple directions, with many fronts erupting simultaneously. When the other fire departments arrived to help, their hose connections did not match up to Oakland's unique couplings, so most proved to be useless.

In Hiller Highlands, Virgina Smith put the leash on her big twelve-year-old dog, Dudley. They had to get out and get out fast. Her narrow street, Charing Cross Road, was choked with cars and with people running down from the winding streets behind her home. The smoke grew increasingly thick. Her husband, Stan, was playing golf and might not even be aware of the fire.

Dudley was a stray who had appeared at the Smith's door one day, starving and needing medical attention. They fed him and took him immediately to a veterinarian who treated him for pneumonia. Virginia visited the mixed breed dog every day. No one claimed the dog, so the Smiths adopted him. By the time of the fire, Dudley had been with the Smiths for seven years. Virginia and Stan were animal lovers, who regularly bought fifty pound sacks of dog food to feed the raccoons who lived in the wooded area around their home. Dudley was especially attached to Virginia, refusing to let her out of his sight, even if she was just going into another room.

Stan Smith saw the plume of smoke in the southern sky from the golf course, but thought it was just another brush fire. It did not alarm him until someone repeated a news bulletin about how the fire was spreading in the hills near the Smith's home. Stan Smith knew then that he had to get back to his wife, but by that time, Hiller Highlands was engulfed in flames. He could not get anywhere near his house because of all the people fleeing. Stan could only watch for his wife of thirty-two years. He looked only for women with dogs, for he knew that Virginia would never leave without Dudley.

Far up on the hillside above, Virginia made it as far as a neighbor's driveway, before she was overcome by the acrid smoke.

Along the same street, Charing Cross Road, Teresa Berkeley's parents knew that they had to flee. With only moments, they called for their daughter's dog, Timothy, but he did not respond. Teresa was not home that day. As they left, they closed the garage door, hoping to shut out the flames and save their townhouse.

Nearby, Kelli Smith slept soundly until her mother, Terri Hensley, telephoned her. Terri had heard the news report of the fire while driving to the family business and wanted Kelli to leave the house. Kelli told her that there was no fire at the house, but her mother insisted that she leave. The bedrooms in their home were on the lowest level on the steeply sloping lot, so Kelli had to go upstairs two more levels to reach the garage. There was a little bit of smoke beginning to come in the windows, so Kelli closed them. Her black and white cat, Max, scooted past her on the stairs, and hid under her bed. On the next level, Kelli closed all of the windows as well. She knew that it was best to close up the house and keep the smoke out. She had no doubt that the fire department was on the way and would have it extinguished in no time. She turned on the foyer light so the firemen could see the house through the smoke, which was getting thicker and blacker. She worried about Max, but knew that she had best get out. Kelli entered the garage and was relieved that the electronic garage-door opener still worked. When the door opened she saw that the bushes next to the house had caught fire. As she backed out, she went to her left, although her parents always went to the right. It was a move that would probably save her life. To the right was the intersection of Charing Cross Road where many people had already died. Kelli had to crouch down in her car to avoid the intense heat as she shot past the flames that were taking over her street. She thought of Max, locked inside the house, and prayed that the fire department would get there in the next few seconds. She knew that she couldn't go back for him and hated the fact that she hadn't tried to get hold of him, but it had been only smoke as she had come upstairs; she had not imagined that it could be anything like this until she emerged from the garage. She took one last look at the narrow street in her rear view mirror and felt the terror of the disaster well up within her as she watched the flames engulf her neighborhood.

Dorothy Sparks had just returned to her home on Starview Court from her walk with Nellie, her dog, and Gus, her cat. She and her husband, Bob, who are both in their seventies, had just settled in to read the Sunday newspaper when they heard a fire engine. Dorothy had seen smoke to the north of them when she was on the walk, but hadn't paid much attention to it. She thought of it as just another brush fire. They heard voices outside and went to investigate. The fire looked like it was coming towards them, so Bob joined the neighbors in hosing down the connected townhouses while Dorothy went around the corner to see where the fire was coming from.

A neighbor hurrying down the street on foot shouted, "A policeman on Charing Cross told me that the fire is out of control and we should take what we need and evacuate." Dorothy returned home and told Bob.

As Dorothy gathered a few necessities upstairs, Bob raced in shouting that the house across the street had caught fire. They picked up Nellie, but couldn't find Gus. Downstairs, the smoke alarm was ringing and their home was filling with smoke. They called for Gus again, but there was no response.

Outside, showers of sparks rained down on them and the sun was obliterated by the dense smoke. Dorothy described it as "walking through a rocket on the Fourth of July." Bob's arm was burned and Dorothy's sweater caught fire. They were forced to leave their car that had their possessions in it, but escaped in their other car. A last attempt to locate Gus proved pointless. He was nowhere to be found. They put on the headlights and drove through the darkness, weaving along, avoiding abandoned cars. Instead of being in the clear air by the time they reached Hiller Drive, they found more fire. It had leapt ahead and around them.

Not far away, Noreen Cardinale and Bobby Wagoner remained at their home until the last possible minute frantically searching for their three cats and trying to save whatever they could. Their roommate, Steven, had corralled his own cat a couple of minutes earlier, but no one had seen any of the others since early that morning.

The wind whipped the flames, encircling their street. Nearby, crackling structures collapsed in a gigantic panorama of destruction on the adjacent hillsides. The pandemonium and immediacy forced them to abandon their search and flee. Noreen looked back through the thickening smoke hoping to see one of their cats, but instead she watched a sheet of flames sweep over the shake roof of their house and devour it.

From downtown Berkeley, Bill Rogers saw the huge column of smoke as he emerged from the gym. It was not quite to his house from what he could tell, but very close. He and Bud proceeded home. Bill worried about his mother, Nancy. The streets leading from the hillsides were choked with traffic. Bill could see that the hillside behind the Claremont Hotel was ablaze. Although his home was on Contra Costa Road on the other side of Highway 24, the smoke was billowing in that direction. The normal routes home were blocked, but since Bill had lived there all of his life, he knew the back ways to get home. Indirect routes got him most of the way there, but he was forced to leave his car on a side street and walk with Bud the final quarter mile. When he arrived, the neighborhood was dark from the ovehanging cloud of smoke. It looked as if the fire had reached this side of the highway. Bill and Bud ran up to the house, but Nancy was not there, although her car was in the garage. Bill pulled the Toyota out of the garage and across the driveway and left it running. Then he grabbed the garden hose and climbed up onto the roof.

He fought the embers that landed on the roof, squirting each one of them with the garden hose. The houses on the street caught fire all around him. He looked down from the roof calling to Bud, and the dog barked back to him. Minutes passed and the embers increased. The house next door caught fire and Bill tried to douse the flames with the hose, but it was no use. When that house exploded, Bill knew he had to flee. He got off the roof and called for Bud, but there was no response from the dog. Bill stayed close by the running car shouting with all of his strength. He decided he might find the dog farther down the road. All of the homes on Contra Costa Road were on fire now. The smoke and heat were intense. Bill did not see the dog as he raced down the center of the street, and came to the convergence of Buena Vista, Golden Gate, and Acacia Roads.

Everyone from the immediate neighborhood had congregated in the large open space. Nancy Rogers suddenly heard her car coming down the road, but couldn't imagine who was driving it. When she saw her son, whom she had believed to be miles away and perfectly safe, coming out of the disaster, her heart sank. Bill ran to her and hysterically explained about Bud and the houses exploding and the walls of flame, and how he had tried, really tried to save their home. He thought maybe Bud had preceded him to this safer site, but Nancy had not seen the dog.

One of the people in the small crowd, Jay Stewart, had also made a last-minute escape. A friend had come over, banging on the door to make sure that Jay would get out of his house. As many others had done that day, Jay had gone about his usual Sunday routine, and was unaware of the fire until he opened the door. The backdrop behind his friend said it all. Jay's only thought was to get his dog, Chad, but unknown to Jay, a neighbor had already opened the gate and let Chad loose, not knowing Jay was inside. Wearing only a pair of shorts and sandals, Jay Stewart joined the others near the old oak tree that stood in the center of the intersection.

Caryn Gottlieb continued towards Santa Cruz. Instead of listening to a favorite tape as was her habit when she took a long drive, she instead tuned in to an AM radio station. Forty-five miles south of San Francisco she heard the first reports of the fire. The parameters given were right in her own neighborhood. She gasped and pulled the car to the side of the road. She had been right. Something terrible was happening.

At her home, her housemate, Linda, was reading in the living room, looking forward to a long, quiet afternoon. She noticed that the carpet was a funny color. Turning to look out the picture window at her back, she could not believe what she saw. The entire sky was red-orange to the east of her. Not wasting any time, Linda grabbed the three cats and her schoolbooks and put them into her small pickup truck. Zeb promptly jumped out the open passenger's-side window that Linda had forgotten to close. She tried to corral him, but he dashed down the side of the house into the blackberry thicket. She had only moments left to make a crucial decision. The fire was raging right in front of her and Zeb had disappeared down a steep slope into thick bushes. She hopped into her vehicle and left, afraid to think about Zeb's fate.

At her home on Alvarado Road, close by the Claremont Hotel, Kristine Barret-Davis became increasingly alarmed as she saw the smoke appear over the ridge at the back of the canyon in which she lived. Among her first thoughts were to get her black and white cat, Disney, but she could not find her. In frustration, she looked everywhere. Disney had been on the deck at the rear of the house that morning. The news reports had Kristine worried. The fire seemed to be getting out of control. Everyone nearby was evacuating, but Kristine held on, still searching for the elusive, slender cat.

Nearby Kristine's home, Dick and Xenia Lee's neighbors did not hesitate to try to save the Lee's three animals: two dogs and a cat. They broke into the gracious Monterey Colonial home that had been in Dick's family for generations, and set off the burglar alarm. They managed to get Gipsy, a six-year-old Brittany Spaniel, but Oscar, a black Labrador eluded them. The cat was never seen. Taking only Gipsy, and none of the Lee's possessions, they raced away from the property. A short while later, as they drove away, the wife turned to see if the dog was all right and found her happily eating the top to the newlywed's wedding cake that the bride had sentimentally saved among her treasured possessions as they fled their own home.

The wildfire became a firestorm, a tall pillar of ferocious frenzy that reached into the sky for hundreds of feet. It pulled in the strong winds at tree-top level, robbing them of oxygen. This rich replacement air mixed in with the burning fuel. The burning embers, or firebrands, hurled out of the top of the pillar and were scattered by the fickle winds. The firestorm created its own wind as well, increasing the spread of the flames. Given the exceptionally dry conditions and the terrain and landscaping, there was virtually nothing to stop it.

Homeowners repeatedly had been asked to remove the dry brush from around their homes but many had not done so, providing the fuel to kindle their homes. The area is heavily forested with trees that have suffered during the extended six years of drought in California, hence providing more fuel. All things considered, though, it does not really make any difference during a firestorm. Everything that stood in its path was incinerated. The temperature of the fire was estimated at over two thousand degrees, the temperature of a crematorium. Even those homes with the fire retardant roofs burned up as quickly as those with traditional shingles. It did not matter what precautions had been taken, it all burned.

The cinders ignited the tree tops which ignited neighboring tree tops in a continuous chain. The firebrands first land on the roof of a house or in the landscaping around it or shower down upon both. The house is then engulfed in flames. The flames suck oxygen out of the house, exploding it as they do so. In moments, only the frame remains visible, a ghostly silhouette. Then the flames gain momentum and grow twice as high as the home, shooting skyward and sending more firebrands towards the next structure.

The sun is obliterated by the smoke. First, it becomes a strange reddish orange color when the smoke is fairly light, giving a surrealistic quality to the landscape. It is followed by the eerie glow of the flames and thicker, denser, choking smoke as the fire moves closer.

Within minutes of the beginning of the fire, the Oakland and Berkeley fire departments found themselves overwhelmed. There was confusion about which addresses were in which city's jurisdiction. Additional cities around the Bay were called upon for help, many responding immediately. By afternoon, the proportions of the fire were already beyond comprehension, and were still growing. The hillside behind the Claremont Hotel was ablaze. The hotel, a landmark since its creation, was renovated in 1989. It has become a deluxe resort and spa with a heritage carefully preserved by the surrounding community. Many local families traditionally celebrate holidays such as Easter or Thanksgiving in the pleasant surroundings.

This Sunday was like all the others at the Claremont. An elegant brunch was being served. The guests commented on what a beautiful day it was—the view of San Francisco Bay was unsurpassed from the terrace because of the wind having whisked away any traces of smog. No one was aware of the fire that was behind the hillside which rises up behind the hotel, until the sky was stained an unnatural orange. It became redder as the smoke thickened. At 12:15 p.m., the order was given to evacuate the hotel. The houses that perched on the hillside looking down on the Claremont were already on fire, and it was spreading rapidly. Every few seconds, another house ignited.

Sometime near noon, Kristine Barrett-Davis was forced to evacuate, still not having found Disney. She left the sliding door to the deck open, though she felt odd about it in case she had to be away for a night or two, and she was also concerned about the smoke damage. After all, the local stations were asking people to close up their homes, and if their pets were inside, to be sure to leave enough food and water for twenty-four hours. Kristine reassured herself that this was just a temporary evacuation. She'd probably be home tonight.

Jan Jacot thought that it was unusual that a neighbor would be using the fireplace on such a warm, gorgeous California day. She sat at her computer composing the letter which was her only task on this otherwise leisurely Sunday. Then she heard distant sirens and some voices outside her home. She went to investigate and found a "tremendous blackness which obliterated the sun." Something very serious was happening and not very far away from her home on Manchester Road. Following the examples of her neighbors up the hillside behind her, she climbed up on her roof and spent twenty minutes hosing it down. The sky was blackening more when the police cars rolled down the streets bellowing with their bullhorns "evacuate now!" One of Jan's cats, Quadri, was nearby. She grabbed him and in the panic that was epidemic throughout the neighborhood, put the cat in the trunk of her classic convertible while she looked for a carrier. When she returned with the appropriate box and opened the trunk, Quadri quickly escaped into her yard. She thought that it was a futile effort, but after many bungled attempts, Jan tackled the cat, who howled and fought furiously. For a moment Jan feared she had used too much force and had hurt the poor animal in her desperate attempt to save it, but the cat had calmed down when placed in the carrier. When Jan had been up on her roof, she had noticed the neighbor's little poodle out in their back yard. She jumped the four foot high hedges to try to catch the terrifed animal, but he would not allow her to get him. Feeling defeated that she could not rescue the dog and her other cat, C.T., Jan took a few possessions and left.

The fire department took a stand—if the Claremont caught fire, it would certainly sweep into the flatter part of town, just below the hotel. The grove of trees just behind the hotel were burning like so many candles on a birthday cake. The guests scrambled to leave, joining the now thousands of others who were streaming off the hillside.

12:15 p.m. to midnight

The crews, aided by hundreds of volunteers, tried to save what they could, but it was quickly becoming clear that the rampage was out of control. The people inhabiting the areas that had appeared to be safe became increasingly concerned as the fire jumped Highway 24, and Highway 13 was closed. Oakland, although it is a major city, has only two channels on their internal radio system, further hampering efforts as the fire erupted on additional fronts. Their new Fire Chief, Lamont Ewell, had only been on the job a few months, coming from Detroit, an area very different from California.

House after house caught fire. People stared in disbelief, fleeing at the last possible second as their cherished homes ignited. Many left literally with just the clothes on their backs.

Diana Ragen watched the sky darken near her home. She would not be caught by this disaster. Methodically, and calmly, Diana packed her things and those of her two children, Kelly and Kacie, who were ten and seven. She watched the helicopters circle overhead and took pictures of them. They dropped their token splashes of water closer to her home with every trip. Diana's ex-husband and current fiancé, Hamed, both showed up with their trucks. Diana had them filled to capacity in very little time. She turned off the gas, and stood there wondering what to take out of the attic. Her neighbors were watching the flames race closer. They asked Diana what she was doing.

"Look over there," she told them, motioning towards the firestorm. "I'm packing."

"What will you do if your house doesn't burn?" they asked.

Nonplussed, Diana answered, "I'll unpack."

Their three cats, Pumpkin, Samantha, and Sundae, were still missing, although the family looked everywhere for them.

In London, England, it was after midnight. Phil Stanley, a resident of Gravatt Drive, and his housemate, George Perko, were asleep in their hotel room, when Phil was awakened by an explosion that rattled the windows and shook his bed. Very shortly after that, another explosion rocked the hotel. Phil thought that the IRA had set off a bomb, as they frequently do in London. George slept through it, and when Phil mentioned it the next morning over breakfast, George had no recollection of it. A check with the front desk at the hotel revealed no activity of any sort which Phil had described. Upon learning of the fire later that day and the loss of their home, Phil realized that the explosion he had experienced had happened at the same time as the explosion of his house thousands of miles away. Their Siamese mix cat, Marduk, (named for the storm god of Babylon), had been acting strangely for the two weeks prior to their trip. Normally an indoor cat, Marduk refused to come inside and they had to start feeding him outside.

All across the hills, people panicked as the firestorm devoured their homes. Some had warning, some did not. There was no stopping the fire until the winds died out. Its swath of destruction across the East Bay Hills was beyond comprehension. The air force took infrared aerial photographs to determine exactly which streets were lost. Primary reports showed hundreds of homes had burned in the first few hours.

On Charing Cross Road, Officer John Grubensky, thirty-two, found himself hemmed in by the fire as it roared towards him. People looked to him to lead them to safety and he tried his best, but the smoke thickened and the abandoned automobiles clogged the road. There was no way out. He tried to lead five people through the smoke, eventually crawling on his hands and knees in what little clear air was left. But they all were overcome. Officer Grubensky's radio lay near his body, still in the "on" position, as the department futilely tried to reach him.

Nearby, Virginia Smith lay dead, the faithful Dudley standing guard over her.

The fire swept through the verdant canyons, up hills, across the narrow streets. There was no telling which way it would turn, as the wind pushed first in one direction, then in another a few seconds later.

Norma Armon ran throughout her Mediterranean-style home opening every closet, cabinet, door, and window in case Charmian was hiding. She wanted the cat to have every chance to escape. Norma's son-in-law, Jon Golding had hosed down evey inch of the house and lawn in order to protect it. His wife of eight months, Carla, Norma's daughter, helped her search for Charmian as they packed photo albums and clothes. Even while she was placing the albums into the trunk of her daughter's car, Norma was certain, like so many other residents of the hillsides, that the house wasn't going to burn. She took the albums because that was what she had always seen people in the movies doing during such a disaster. They re-recorded their answering machine message to say that they had evacuated. Most of all, they continued their frantic search for Charmian.When the nearby electric tower exploded like a Roman candle on the Fourth of July, they were forced to flee.

"Even as we left," Carla explained, "we thought that the house and the cat would be all right." They left with very little because, as Carla pointed out, "this is the United

States, and they're going to put out the fire any minute now."

Not far from Norma's house, Ron and Carol Hofmann searched futilely for their five cats. The next door neighbors were away and their thirteen-year-old son was home alone. Ron and Carol made sure that he was ready to leave with them and managed to find his two cats and securely place them in carriers. One last quick look around and they had no other choice but to leave. Ron and Carol had Mandy, their small older dog, with them and nothing else.

Wildlife fled along with the rest. Deer crashed through yards and when encountering a human in the pandemonium, retreated, sometimes with fatal consequences. Raccoons, skunks, possums, wild rabbits and mice were seen taking off in all directions. All had one thing on their minds, whether human or animal: survival. Much of the wildlife fled towards the open space preserves at the crest of the hills and into Contra Costa County, although deer were spotted in the very heavily inhabited area around the University of California. Ty Phillips, a meter reader for East Bay Municipal Utilities District or "East Bay MUD" as it is commonly called, knew that there was a daschund puppy that was home alone. Its owners were away. The puppy had repeatedly barked and barked at Ty as he made his rounds earlier that week. Without another thought for his own safety, Ty drove through the hills that he knew so well, dodging the onslaught of cars coming down the hillside in the opposite direction. He reached the house, and the puppy, grateful to be rescued did not utter a peep as Tom carried him away to safety.

Up in Hiller Highlands, three people found themselves trapped by the fire. Although it enclosed them for over an hour, they had miraculously survived. The moment there was a break ahead of them, the trio decided to run. As they ran down Charing Cross Road, they found Dudley guarding Virginia's body. The fire rampaged several stories' high around them, and the escape gap was narrowing. The sounds of the power lines snapping and whizzing overhead and the abandoned automobiles exploding as the fire ignited their gas tanks made the area sound like a blitzkrieg. Frantically, they unwound the leash from Virginia Smith's wrist and attempted to lead Dudley to safety, but he stood like a statue, rooted to the ground. They tugged and pulled and coaxed, but Dudley would not budge. The fireball bore down on them, there was no time to waste, but they were determined to save Dudley's life. They alternately pulled and pushed the reluctant dog along. Dudley kept stopping and looking back at his mistress. Finally, they were all safe. They rushed Dudley to the Berkeley Dog and Cat Hospital, telling the staff "We just couldn't leave him. We couldn't leave him." Dudley's fur was singed and his paw pads were burned, but the dog seemed to be in otherwise fine shape. However, his depression was obvious, and it deepened over the next few hours. The staff attempted to call the number on his tag, but it was out of order, as were thousands of other telephones in the two cities. They knew that the woman trying to save him had died, but they hoped that maybe other family members might have survived and would claim the big, loving well-behaved dog. The staff at the clinic did what they could for Dudley's physical wounds, but there was nothing that they could do for his spirit.

The three survivors' unselfishness in rescuing an unknown, helpless animal that afternoon was only overshadowed by Dudley's own devotion and valor in choosing to stay at Virginia's side, protecting her lifeless form even as the choking blanket of smoke closed around him.

Thousands of miles away in Denmark, Esther Rasmussen parked her rental car, and securely locked the doors as she visited her mother on one of her frequent journeys to her homeland. Afterwards, as she left with her nephew to return to her sister's home in a neighboring village, Esther was shocked to find a cat in her car. The doors were still locked. She asked her mother about the cat, but she had never seen the cat before. Esther asked around, and finally released the cat. She told her family, "This is a message from my cat, Mr. Fox. Either he is telling me good-bye or that he is all right." An hour later, Esther was alerted by a family member to turn on CNN. She watched in horror as the news broadcast told of the destruction and fury of the firestorm in Oakland. The camera panned in on a home on fire in the Oakland Hills— her home.

Jimmy Reina and Elaine Gerber made it up to their Capricorn Avenue home in the Broadway Terrace section in record time in spite of the steady stream of evacuees who sometimes took up both sides of the streets as they fled downhill.

As the black cloud grew above them, they began their frantic search for the three cats, Mookie, Simi and Mamalucci. First to be found was Mookie. They placed him in a carrier. Jimmy found Mamalucci, Mookie's twin brother, outside and brought him in and put him in the bathroom, but in the panic, Mamalucci, whose name in Italian means "crazy or wild one," escaped from his confinement and got outside. Jimmy chased him up and down the hillside behind their home, but Mamalucci appropriately lived up to his name and ran amuck through the trees, in sight of Jimmy, but refusing to come near him. Simi, who was fourteen years old, was nowhere to be found. At Jimmy's insistence, Elaine reluctantly fled with Lido, their fourteen-year-old ailing poodle, and Mookie.

Jimmy remained at the property for about another three hours, clearing brush and hosing down every surface that was exposed, in hopes of saving their home. He searched and searched for the two missing cats, but they had vanished. He was crestfallen when a helicopter pilot ordered him to evacuate. He was the sole occupant of the entire area when he drove away, empty-handed. By his nature, the mischievous Mamalucci had placed himself in incredible danger.

Christine O'Connell left her two-year-old son Scott with her sister. The quiet afternoon that was to be spent shopping was truncated when they heard someone in the shopping mall talk about the fire. They were about twenty minutes from home, but while driving back, they could see the thick cloud of rising black smoke. Christine's sister's home was no where near the area, but the parent's home was in the same block as Christine's, so the baby was sent off with his aunt for safety. Although the O'Connell's lived in the Broadway Terrace area, the reports that it was spreading sent Christine flying up the stairs. "The cat, the cat" were the first words to her husband, John. He grabbed her by the shoulders and told her to look on the floor. Their ten-year-old cat, Roscoe, was already in the carrier. John had also gathered some things and had put them nearby. "What about the other cats?" she asked. The feral mother and two kittens who had moved in with the O'Connell's were not to be found. They had only been touched once, when John and Christine had trapped them and had them spayed. "Even if they were sitting right there," John pointed to the rear deck of the house where the cats lived, "you know that we couldn't catch them. I'm sure they were out of here at the first whiff of smoke." Christine agreed and started the laborious process of deciding what to take. The radio and television blared doomsday reports. The O'Connell's decided to take their personal treasures, just to be on the safe side. As if in a dream, Christine went into every room of their home and took things, but only those things at eye-level, not looking up or down.

That morning, Yves and Dawn Mottier left for breakfast in Berkeley a few miles from their Grandview Drive home. When the news of the fire reached them, their only thought was of their seven cats who were indoors. Yves and Dawn, a registered nurse, had to abandon their car and use old hiking trails to avoid the roadblocks that were preventing people from entering the area.

Eventually, they also abandoned the hiking trails, and with their clothes and skin ripped by thorns from plowing through the underbrush, the Mottiers reached their rented home. The fire was almost there and time was of the essence. Yves had left his house keys in the car, so he picked up the barbecue and hurled it through the front window. He thought to himself, "This had better be a real emergency or the landlord is really going to be angry." The cats were too spooked to catch, so Yves and Dawn raced through the house, opening all the doors and windows in order to give the cats a chance to escape. When the smoke became too thick to see or to breathe any longer, the Mottiers fled, not bothering to grab any objects as they left. They had given the seven terrified cats "a fighting chance." At least they had not been left to burn to death in a locked house.

GeorgeAnn Hemingway-Proia had waited far beyond the last possible minute to leave her home near the intersection of Fairlane and Swainland. She was so reluctant to give up her search for her black and white cat, Casey, that a police officer literally had to pick her up and carry her, struggling, out of the house, while another officer escorted her husband. Their month-old kitten, Ginger, was already loaded into a carrier in the car. Ginger had watched them with kitten fascination from a ring-side seat on their bed as GeorgeAnn and Don raced about the home they had occupied for less than a month, gathering important papers and mementos. Forced by the police to leave, GeorgeAnn and Don drove as slowly as possible down the streets of the Broadway Terrace area, hoping for some sight of Casey. Every home around them was now engulfed in flames.

On and on the firestorm raged. Every few seconds, another home was consumed by the angry flames. It seemed as if it would devour the entire East Bay before it ended, and then the winds lost their strength and the fire looked as though it might be subdued. The fire department had designated which homes could be saved and fought long and hard with a corps of volunteers to do so. Because of the brush and trees or the situation of the house, many were deemed to be lost before the fire had even touched them.

Jimmy Reina found Elaine and Lido and Mookie at the prearranged address of a good friend of theirs. They watched the news coverage, as did so many others. Finally, Jimmy could stand it no longer. They could see the fire ravaging the neighborhoods from the safe house. Jimmy could not just sit on a front porch and watch it all burn. He knew that he had to try again to rescue the cats they had left behind. He left, driving almost under a spell, watching the orange and red flames race from house to house. He took roads whose names were totally unfamiliar to him, winding his way through Piedmont, a city adjacent to Oakland, whose magnificent homes lay in the fire's path. Piedmont is next to the Montclair District, on the western side of Highway 13, now closed to traffic. Jimmy found himself on a hillside overlooking the Montclair area, watching the fire relentlessly and rapidly spread. He stood transfixed. After an hour and a half, he decided that it was useless to try to get back to his house, and he started back to the safe house where Elaine and the dog and cat were waiting for him. Suddenly, he realized that he was behind the fire and police barriers, looking out over the city, not up at it. A wrong turn had put him into the evacuated area. Jimmy began to recognize some of the street names. He cautiously crept up back roads to their house, the only light guiding him being the eerie orange glow from the approaching inferno. With immense relief, Jimmy saw that their home was still there. He flew up the eighty stairs to the front door, unlocked it and found the flashlight that he always kept on the mantle for emergencies. He used it to scan the living room, and found Simi, the fourteen-year-old solid gray cat, comfortably curled up asleep on Lido's dog bed. The carrier had been left in the living room and Jimmy wasted no time in placing Simi inside. The telephone was still operational, so he called Elaine to tell her the great news.

He opened the door and called for the remaining cat, Mamalucci, then he saw the cat calmly sitting on the fence, watching the flames on an adjacent hillside with the same transfixion with which Jimmy had watched them earlier that evening. Jimmy knew that he would have only one chance to grab Mamalucci. Barely breathing, he cautiously crept forward trying to be as natural as possible and not alarm the cat any further. With one lightning-quick movement, Jimmy lunged. He caught Mamalucci by the tail, dangling over the other side of the fence. The cat made every feline attempt that he could to escape—spitting, hissing, and clawing, but Jimmy refused to relinquish his grasp, no matter how violently Mamalucci fought to get away. Jimmy and Mamalucci wrestled the entire way into the house, and careful not to let Simi escape from the carrier, Jimmy dropped the berserk Mamalucci inside and slammed the carrier shut. He was elated! He had finally captured all of their pets. He ran down the stairs with the squirming, frightened cats in the carrier, jumped in his car, and fled down the darkened, narrow hillside streets, leaving their home behind.

That night, as she was driving to her home in Richmond, Doll Stanley, a dedicated employee of In Defense of Animals, saw the pall of smoke that billowed over the two cities. "I just know there are animals up there," she thought as she kept driving towards the fire instead of taking a turn-off toward her home. Night was beginning to fall. Doll had been out of the area the entire day, having researched reports of a bear poacher in the Sierra Nevada mountains of California. The first she knew of the fire was when she heard a caustic disc jockey make a glib comment about "roasting marshmallows." The news reports gave Doll a more accurate idea of what was happening.

Animals had been found all during the day throughout the city. One dog, found in San Leandro, many miles to the south, was so covered with soot that it took six baths to uncover its real yellow color. No one would have believed a dog would have covered so much territory if it had not been for that obvious evidence. Not only did "fire animals" run from the flames, but those pets on the peripheral areas fled as well. The city of Oakland took no chances and forced the evacuation as far west as College Avenue, so many more animals were actually affected than just those whose homes were burned. A number of veterinary hospitals also had to be evacuated that afternoon. Because the smoke was borne by the winds as far south as San Jose, a distance of fifty miles, the animals in the cities immediately surrounding Oakland and Berkeley would have been in a panic as well.

Even under the best of conditions, if an animal is reluctant to do something, it will struggle against you, no matter how docile it normally is. Coupled with the owner's panic and the sounds of the helicopters, air tankers, and sirens, many pets, especially cats, escaped their owners' grasp and began their own evacuation plan.

Nancy Rogers and her son Bill knew that their house was gone. They had watched from the convergence of the three roads as long as they could and then they were forced to flee further downhill. Nancy thought about Princess, her calico cat. Had she died in the inferno? No, something within Nancy told her that if any cat had survived, it had been Princess. Despite her dainty name, she was one tough cat. "Matter of time," Nancy thought. They had to find shelter for the night, so Nancy suggested that they find a pay telephone. The nearest one that she could think of was at her church, which was not in the affected area. They drove away, still looking for Bud. Bill was inconsolable. It tore him up to think that Bud had perished in the flames, but maybe he had died instantly when one of the neighboring houses had exploded, and he had not suffered. The furious sound of the flames was so loud that Bill had not heard a yelp or a cry.

They reached the church, over a mile and a half from the present edge of the fire. Bill accompanied his mother to the pay phone, but they stopped in their tracks when they saw the yellow dog sitting on the church steps. At first Bill thought that it was some sort of weird apparition that he was seeing from breathing so much smoke. He stood and blinked and looked again, dumbfounded. Bill and the dog ran to greet each other. Bud had gone to a location that he had been to only once before, more than a year ago, and waited patiently for his family to meet him there. He seemed to have known that they would be there to find him even before they had decided to go there themselves.

At two a.m. on Monday morning, Ted Young, who had been valiently struggling to save his parents' home, descended through the night, driving slowly and talking to his wife on the cellular phone in his truck, describing the eerie surroundings. As he drove down Swainland Avenue, he passed Norma Armon's property. A cat yowled so loudly that Ted's wife Karen heard it over the phone.

"What was that?" she asked.

Ted stopped and investigated. "It's a cat, more dead than alive," he replied.

"Well, bring it home with you."

They argued over the cat that sat crying on the sidewalk. Ted really disliked cats and claimed that it would maul him if he tried to pick it up. His wife told him adamantly not to come home without the cat. Karen sat up all night tending to the creature. The cat's fur was burned off and it had suffered severe smoke inhalation. The paw pads and ears were almost burned off, too. It would be a miracle if the cat lasted until she could take it in for veterinary care first thing in the morning.

At three o'clock in the morning, Don and GeorgeAnn crouched silently in bushes in front of a house just outside the perimeter of the fire. Each wore a backpack with cat food and water to leave out for their cat, Casey. They knew from all of the reports that their home had not survived the inferno. But their fears that Casey was alone and frightened and possibly injured, drove them to their clandestine search for him. They had wet towels wrapped around their faces to filter the acrid air, which was almost overwhelming.

Each home site was now reduced to glowing red embers outlined by the house's foundation. As they crept forward, GeorgeAnn and Don could see tiny pinpoints of white light on the hillside. Cautiously approaching one of the lights, they were surprised to discover that it was the inside dome light of a police car. They knew now exactly where each car was, and figured that the accompanying patrolman would not be too far away. Cutting across the foot-high piles of ash and debris in the yards, the couple cautiously trekked up the hillside. They inched forward, using their flashlights for only a few seconds at a time in order not to be seen by the police. All around them were downed electric power lines.

It took them over an hour to reach their home. When they were within a few yards of it they were amazed by what they saw. All around them the foundations of their neighbors' homes glowed red, yet their home was still standing. A glimpse of moonlight revealed that the roof and siding had burned away, as had all of their yard. The windows had blown out, too. In astonishment, they opened the door. Don wondered if the house was a false facade, like a movie set, and he prepared himself for the emptiness they might find. But the rooms were intact. Their house was the only one in at least a six-block radius to have survived.

The began a room-by-room search for Casey. They called softly for him, keeping their flashlights low. In Don's office they heard a faint meow. Calling again, they began searching carefully in the enveloping darkness, but couldn't find him. They risked a check outside the exploded window, but the weak cry seemed to be coming from inside the house.

At last they isolated the cries to a corner of the office where a filing cabinet stood. GeorgeAnn opened the cabinet door and then slid open the bottom drawer and Casey popped out, somewhat confused, but otherwise unharmed by his sojourn.

In their flight GeorgeAnn and Don had opened the cabinet to retrieve important papers, and Casey had evidently dived into the drawer when their backs were turned.

Casey ate with gusto before GeorgeAnn and Don happily trundled him off in his carrier. They left the house just before dawn, carefully retracing their steps out of the firestorm zone. Their secret mission had been successful.

Part Two:
THE RESCUES

Monday, October 21, 1991— 5 a.m. to 12:00 p.m.

The first rays of sun that morning revealed a landscape that looked more lunar than earthly. It was Ground Zero— miles of ashes that looked as though a nuclear explosion had occurred on the hillsides. The police barricades were well guarded and the crowds began to gather at them, hoping for a glimpse of their homes. No one was allowed into the area because downed power lines and still smoldering embers constituted a real threat to safety. The rescue crews had come from all over California and began combing the streets for any signs of life or human remains.

Across the once verdant canyons and heavily forested hillsides stood chimneys, like tombstones for each home. Lining the streets were the charred hulks of automobiles. The intense heat had melted the chrome from them into puddles that formed in the melting asphalt on the street. Tires were reduced to only frayed steel bands. Everywhere were blocks and blocks of ashes. Ironically, a real estate company's "For Sale" sign swung in the breeze that had calmed down a day too late. The sign, barely scorched, now advertised an empty lot with only a foundation and some brick steps. Here and there an identifiable chunk of metal was recognized as a water heater or a clothes dryer. Wrought iron handrailing survived, guides along steps that led to emptiness. The fire had burned everything. The few people allowed into the zone were escorted by the police, driven in squad cars in order to see for themselves that their once cherished homes were gone. One woman recalled looking for her cast iron bathtub, sure that it at least would have survived, but it had not. There was a six-inch-high ash pile across her lot. The fire had reached crematorium temperatures. Because of the terrain, many of the remains of the homes built on the steep hillsides tumbled down onto the properties below. These owners were not even allowed the luxury of having an ash pile to comb through.

The first lists of lost streets were published and broadcast, many of them hastily put together from aerial views. The news spread throughout the gathered crowds. The names of streets were whispered over and over, followed by the statement, "All gone."

With keen anxiety, Ethel King waited behind the police barricades to be escorted up to her property. Although she knew that nothing remained of her home, the seventy-year-old widow wanted to look for her cat, Gallagher, and see what was left for herself. Gallagher had been rescued by Ethel's daughter, Diane, in another part of Oakland about a year before. He had been abandoned and the owner of the property threatened to trap him and take him to the pound, but Diane intervened and persuaded her mother to adopt the slender orange cat.

Her next-door neighbor, Muriel, found Ethel in the crowd and told how she had fled, taking only the pillow-case, which she had been changing when she saw the fire. Muriel also told Ethel that Gallagher had scurried down the street alongside of her for part of the distance. Ethel felt indescribable relief at that moment. Now, with renewed hope, she gripped the bar of the barricade. Her little companion was alive. Knowing that Gallagher had escaped, her worst fear passed. Although she was still concerned about his safety after Muriel lost sight of him, Ethel now had a goal on which to focus: find Gallagher.

The grim pilgrimage of survivors had begun. Those who had fled in panic on Sunday returned to wait for the official escort to see what the fire had left. When they got there, they found nothing except blackened ashes. Lifetimes of memories had been incinerated.

The Alameda County Veterinarian's Association had been preparing a disaster plan during the aftermath of the October 1989 Loma Prieta Earthquake. It was not fully operational yet, but when the firestorm erupted, Dr. Rene Gandalfi, the president of the association, knew that what they had would have to suffice. That morning, the first steps were taken to establish a formalized rescue effort for the companion animals that had been affected by the firestorm. The Oakland Animal Shelter and the Oakland and Berkeley SPCAs had been receiving injured cats and dogs throughout the night. Private veterinary hospitals had also accepted animals, some injured, others who had been evacuated with their owners and had no home to go to.

The crews needed to go over the entire zone before the residents could be re-admitted. There were still over a dozen people on the missing list—those who were known to be up in the affected area, but had not been located at the shelters or through the Red Cross efforts. One of those was Virginia Smith. Stan Smith, her husband, had looked for Virginia all of Sunday afternoon and again on Monday morning. Every time he gave her description, he added that she would have a large dog with her, and gave Dudley's description as well. Stan knew that under no circumstances would Virginia have left without Dudley, nor would she have become separated from him at a shelter. If the shelter refused to take pets, as some had done, Virginia would just go find a shelter or hotel that did accept Dudley. Stan was so insistent about Virginia being with Dudley that he asked for a "lady with a big dog," all in one breath. No one had seen her, nor did they have her name on any list or roster.

Norma Armon was one of the first people at the barricades near her house that morning. She had not slept all night. All she wanted to do was to go feed Charmian, who she thought must be terribly hungry by now. Norma's house was secondary, it was Charmian who had her so worried. She stood at the barricade and pleaded with the officer to let her through. "All I want to do is feed my cat and take her with me." Norma clutched the food can and water jug, not realizing that it was one of the few possessions that she had left. Her home on Swainland Drive had fallen to the flames in mid-afternoon the day before.

Norma Armon's emotions were at a peak, as they had been since the time she evacuated. She knew in her heart that Charmian was still alive. She begged and pleaded and cajoled with anyone who would listen. Escort her up there, watch her every move. She didn't care—she was not a looter. All she wanted to do was to feed her cat! Her pleas were overheard by a photographer from the San Jose *Mer-*

cury-News. He was touched by Norma's story and they struck a deal. He would get her up to her house with his press credentials if she would let him photograph the entire scenario. Norma, an attractive woman in her fifties, was stressed to her all-time worst. She had not slept, she probably looked a wreck, but she did not care. "Take all the pictures you want," the spunky woman told him. "Just get me up to my cat and to my house!"

With great anticipation, they walked up the hill. Norma was running on sheer nerves now, and was anxious to get Charmian out of there. From the lower part of Swainland, she could see that her house was no longer there. She ran ahead, expecting to find Charmian waiting for her, but the cat was not anywhere. Dejectedly, Norma placed the bowls with water and Charmian's favorite food on the walkway after brushing away the cinders. She called and called, but her voice echoed over the empty, charred lots. There was no feline answer. Still Norma knew that she had survived. "Come on," she told the photographer, "I've got to start searching for her. Let's check the shelters."

Governor Pete Wilson toured the area in a helicopter on Monday morning. President Bush declared it a disaster area after a briefing at the White House. Still, no one knew exactly how many were dead, injured, or still missing. The property loss estimate was already close to five billion dollars. The enormity of this disaster was overshadowing anything that had taken place in California except for the 1906 earthquake and fire that destroyed most of San Francisco over three days. If this firestorm had been given that much time, it may well have surpassed the 1906 disaster in terms of property loss. Twenty-eight thousand buildings were destroyed in the 1906 earthquake and fire. The death estimate has never been properly determined, but numbers were in the thousands. San Francisco's disaster eighty-five years prior could be considered two that were linked together. Oakland's tragedies were two years apart.

On Siler Place, a team of paramedics searched the cul-de-sac for any victims. Oddly, the fire had devastated only the south side of the narrow street. Across from smoldering lumps were homes that were untouched. The wind had shifted, driving the flames in another direction. If you stood with your back to the carnage, you would never have known there had been a fire on this quiet lane, for not even the lighter colored homes were smoke-damaged. Espaliered ivy on one house was a bit singed on the edges, but looked like nothing more than too much exposure to direct sun. The delicate trellis on which it grew crisscrossed remained intact.

The two paramedics found what looked to be a pile of rubble, but upon closer inspection, it turned out to be a cat. The pathetic creature was still alive but barely hanging on. They carefully lifted the little survivor and placed it in a box. As they did so, charcoal fell off its tiny body. The paramedics wasted no time in rushing the cat to the nearest veterinarian. They left Siler Place with lights flashing and sirens wailing.

Since they were from out of the area, they drove to the nearest large, busy street in search of a vet. Blocks and blocks later, as traffic cleared out of their path, they found Claremont Animal Hospital on College Avenue. They rushed the cat inside, telling the staff where they had found it and the circumstances. Immediately, Dr. William Frizell attended to the tiny female. Her chances were slim, but she had survived through the night, and, although in shock, her vital signs were good. He found that there had been very little smoke inhalation, which was the best sign of all. Damage to the lungs dangerously weakened an animal, but this cat miraculously had very little lung damage. It was the rest of the injuries that worried Dr. Frizell. Her fur was gone, burned off, except for a few tiny tufts that remained and identified her as a tortoiseshell. Hot tar had dripped down her back, searing her skin in a four-inch diameter patch. Her head was a mass of oozing, bloody pus. A bone was exposed in her nose and another on the tip of her tail. Her tiny paw pads had third degree burns. Her eyelids and most of her ears were missing, yet she clung to life. Bandaged, medicated, and sedated, the cat was placed in an incubator and fed intravenously. Time was on her side. She had survived the first crucial hours outside all night and was still alive. That in itself made the doctor believe that the small cat would pull through. The veterinarian's office called the local shelter and reported her as "Tortoiseshell Female." More than that, they could not tell.

The pet rescue effort through the Alameda County Veterinarian Association was becoming a reality. Because the plan was not fully operational, loose ends still had to be tied up. No one had expected another disaster so soon after the earthquate, and certainly not a fire of this magnitude. The plan had been more geared toward earthquake survival.

The first task was to be sure that communications were set up. A telephone number was arranged through the phone company with multiple lines. Alameda County Veterinary Association contacted a number of animal groups in the area with volunteers who might be called upon to coordinate the rescue. The main goal was to centralize the reports, not to get duplicate information that would waste time and resources, and to get all of the reports from the different shelters.

Patt Shaw spent hours on the telephone at her Orinda home. She had spoken to Dr. Rene Gandalfi earlier in the day. She felt lucky to have two telephone lines to use to help coordinate the pet rescue effort. Patt had been involved in animal causes since the early seventies, and was currently serving on the board of the Volunteers of Contra Costa County as animal liaison. The fire had not jumped the hill and gone east to the wooded canyon where she lived in Orinda, but the streets had been blocked off all that afternoon and Patt had not returned home until late that evening, much to the chagrin of her dog and three cats. She understood the helplessness at being denied access to her home and immediately helped set into motion the first vestiges of the rescue. If the wind had changed ever so slightly, Patt knew that she would be searching for her own pets.

Doll Stanley knew that IDA (In Defense of Animals) in San Rafael, the group that she worked for, would be able to supply a lot of the necessary items and people needed. At a meeting early that morning, Doll and most of the staff prepared to go over to the opposite side of the Bay to begin the search. Everyone was stunned by the devastation and sickened by the bodies of animals that seemed to be everywhere. One of the first that Doll found was that of a large dog, a Bouvier des Flandres. She saw that he had on a collar and tags and removed them, so she could contact the owners and let them know that their dog had perished. Later that day she turned over the collar to Berkeley Humane Society.

That afternoon, Juanita Simpson faced an anguish that was worse for her than losing her home. She had Oliver, her dying cat, whom she had rescued from the ravages of the firestorm the previous day, put to sleep, compounding her enormous loss.

The City of Oakland began implementation of a One Stop Center for the survivors of the firestorm. Located in a former supermarket, it would be the only place that the people would have to go to in order to begin piecing their lives back together. It had a central location in a good neighborhood near the major freeways, parking facilities, and enough room to accommodate hundreds of people.

The Red Cross had a table at the One Stop Center, offering their wide array of relief services. They offered the Pet Rescue half of their space to use near the rear of the building. Thus a formalized rescue had begun, the first of its kind for domestic pets. The start-up costs of the operation for necessities such as film, photocopying, and office supplies were underwritten by an anonymous donor. The rescue effort was a conglomeration of various groups working in conjunction with basic goals in mind: to find and reunite as many pets as possible with their owners, and to help any injured animals. Immediately the press broadcast the story and asked for volunteers. That is how I became involved.

Initially, the entire operation was difficult to locate. There were references to a "Pet Rescue" in the press, but when I tried to find a telephone number through the phone company I was told that there was no such group. I called the Oakland Animal Shelter and learned that In Defense of Animals was handling some of the main coordination of the plan, but when I tried to get their number, directory assistance again couldn't help me. I had to track them down, and found out that they were in Marin County, California, about twenty miles north of the Golden Gate Bridge and across the Bay from where the disaster had occurred.

Monday, 12:00 p.m. to 6:00 p.m.

Jimmy Reina and Elaine Gerber heard shortly after noon that their home had survived the conflagration. The fire had been stopped on their block, and from all reports, their home had come dangerously close to being among those that were lost. Jubilantly, they went off for lunch with the friend who had put them up for the night. The three cats and Lido, their standard poodle, had been disoriented by the break in their routines. Mamalucci cried to get outside, but they would not let him. They might be home by this afternoon, or tomorrow or the next day at the very latest. It saddened them to think of all the loss that their neighbors had experienced, but they celebrated their own good fortune in a quiet manner. Soon they could go home and resume as normal a life as possible.

The residents of Berkeley and Oakland walked around in a state of stunned disbelief. How could this have happened? How could a routine brush fire turn into this monstrous blaze? No one had the answers. On Monday, the officials cautiously declared that the fire was out, except for a few hot spots that had continued to smolder. They predicted that the danger would soon be over if the weather was cooperative and the winds did not resume. The weather was cooler on Monday, which was a relief to all in the area. There were five thousand people estimated to be homeless from the fire. Another five thousand had been evacuated from the peripheral areas. Officials confirmed that the fire had begun in the Grandview neighborhood on Buckingham Boulevard from the embers of the six-acre brush fire.

Later that afternoon, Jimmy Reina and Elaine Gerber got more news: their house had been the last to burn. Their elation turned to grief. At least the animals had been rescued. They would find a new home. Jimmy looked at the most recent list of lost houses. It was true. The house was gone. The last one. How ironic. It was almost comical. What was next? What could be next?

The scene was played out again and again as people were allowed onto their street or given the news at checkpoints set up around the perimeter. Grown men sank to their knees in the piles of ashes that had been their homes and wept openly. Families who had been living the "American Dream" only twenty-four hours previously clung together, sobbing as they saw the smoking ruins that were left. Mementos, family treasures, all lay in ashes at their feet. In Hiller Highlands, the paper cups at the side of the tennis courts were lined up neatly in their dispenser, unscorched by the flames. An insignificant item had been spared, while so many treasures had been incinerated.

Sara Somers sifted through the ashes of her Alpine-style home in the upper Rockridge section that afternoon. The aerial shots showed the wide swath of the destruction. She had no hopes of finding the one thing that she was searching for: her cat, Dave Stewart. She had not been able to find him the previous afternoon and had to evacuate without him. Tearfully, she removed chunks of debris, expecting to find a carcass. She was certain that Dave Stewart was dead. All night she had been haunted by the vision of him burning alive. Suddenly she heard a faint meowing from a grove of charred trees that had been behind her house. Looking up, she smiled as Dave appeared. "This makes everything O.K. now," she sobbed into his fur. "Let the looters have what they can find. I don't care about anything else."

By that afternoon, about fifty animals had been brought into the Oakland SPCA. Several were being treated for burns and smoke inhalation. Photographers rushed in to take pictures of the pets. Some veterinarian hospitals, Claremont Animal Hospital among them, phoned in reports about the pets that they were treating. All graciously offered to take injured animals at no charge, even when the owner was known.

Dogs and cats were not the only animals rescued. There were horse stables up in the unincorporated sections of the hills, out where the land had flattened out enough to accommodate them. Golden Gate Fields, a local racetrack, had put out a media message that it could take horses, and about one hundred had been brought in Sunday night from private stables and a riding academy.

People who had taken their pets out of the path of the fire and now found themselves without a home needed foster care for them while they attempted to restore order to their own lives. The Oakland SPCA's dozen phone lines were kept busy with these tasks since the day before. Many of their volunteers had slept at the shelter. People who could provide foster care came forward in record numbers. They understood that many pets needed a peaceful situation, too.

The community was pulling together in its hours of desperate need. Neighbors were helping neighbors. Strangers offered shelter to those who had lost their homes. The spirit was alive in a city that has had more than its share of urban violence and catastrophe, but had risen above its problems to assist those who had need of help.

Stan Smith received the dreaded news that his wife, Virginia, had perished in the fire. Stan asked about Dudley, but no one had found his body. Stan insisted that Dudley's body must have been near Virginia's. If Virginia had died, Dudley had died. Under no circumstances would Virginia have left Dudley, nor would he have left her. Their devotion was unquestionable. Stan insisted they look again.

Tuesday Morning, October 22, 1991

The news reports were becoming worse and worse. At first it was believed that only hundreds of homes had burned down, but the numbers increased with every broadcast until they reached the thousands. The aerial shots showed the destruction. More streets were added to the lengthy list of those that had been completely lost. After each street name was the notation "gone": a neighborhood's grief summed up in four letters.

On Tuesday morning the new reports were especially grim. The death toll was twenty-one; the missing numbered thirty-seven, and the authorities feared that some of them may not have escaped. More than 2,700 homes and apartments had been gutted. The fire had cut across all classes and demographics. Young and old, affluent and fixed incomes, owners and renters, famous and unknown. One of the unique features of the hills is that a palatial home may be on the same block as a modest bungalow. Now all of the survivors were equal in a sense—no one had anything left.

A state senator and a baseball star, along with noted writers and artists, suffered the devastation along with young families and senior citizens. Most were still in a state of shock. The anger and grief were just beginning to seep into their consciousness. Mayor Elihu Harris of Oakland ordered the city flags to be flown at half-staff for a month to honor those who had lost their lives in the inferno and publicly commended the firefighters, police officers, and volunteers who worked so heroically to extinguish the blaze. Without their efforts, the conflagration might have become far worse than it had.

Up on Swainland Drive, Norma Armon resumed her search for her cat Charmian. She was certain she had survived. It was a feeling that she had down to her core. Still, Norma was overcome with concern about Charmian's welfare. The food she had left the previous day had not been eaten. She placed another paper plate nearby and opened another can of "Charm's" favorite food. She threw the bowl of water onto the blackened earth, and refilled it. Once more she walked along the vacant street calling for Charmian.

The survivors had begun to pull their lives together, if only on a limited basis. Most left with nothing, some with a few important papers or their pets. Nearly everything had to be purchased. Most began with toothbrushes. Their lists for basic necessities expanded as they estimated what they would need. Some still did not know if their homes were gone, intact, or partially ruined. The local hotels were jammed, and most offered a fifty percent discount to the displaced. The Claremont Hotel, spared when the wind shifted, was among the first to help out in this manner. Many of the survivors took up residence there. It was in such close proximity to the cordoned off area, that they could be nearby when they were allowed to return to their homes.

Diana Ragen accepted the news that the home she had inherited from her mother was gone. Her grandmother had originally built on the property in the Broadway Terrace area over sixty years before. Stoically and with a great measure of strength, Diana began the arduous journey of making life as normal as possible for her two children, Kelly and Kacie. Top priority was to locate the three cats, Pumpkin, Samantha, and Sundae.

At one of the animal shelters, Diana found a report about a tortoiseshell female at Claremont Veterinary Hospital. It was the closest match to any of the three cats. It was worth checking out. Diana immediately went to the veterinary hospital and explained her situation. She was told how badly the cat that they had in the incubator was injured. Diana described Pumpkin to the staff, and said she might be able to identify her by an orange patch on one of her toes—the third one on her right foot. A minute later, Dr. Frizell came to the door. "I think you had better come in and look," he said solemnly.

Diana was shocked by the appearance of the cat, but it did not repulse her. Cautiously she leaned closer and the vet showed her the orange toe that Diana had described. A further check also revealed an orange triangular patch on her chin. "It's her, it's really her," she tearfully told the vet, who was also crying as was the rest of the staff. Diana softly called to Pumpkin. The cat raised her head and responded with a feeble but long meow. It was the first sound that anyone had heard from the cat since she had been brought in by the paramedics the previous day. Ironically, Dr. Frizell was Pumpkin's regular veterinarian, but because of her extensive injuries, he had not recognized her. The vet offered slim hope that she would pull through, giving her only about a fifty percent chance for survival. He asked Diana if she wished to have Pumpkin put to sleep.

"Not now, I couldn't," she told the vet. "After what she has survived, she deserves the chance to pull through. She has made it this far, I know she will make it all the way."

"I'm glad that you feel that way. I do, too," he told her. "I'm obligated to give you the option, though. We will do everything possible to save her and to keep her out of pain. You just keep coming, let her know that you're here for her, that you love her. That will aid her recovery in a big way. We'll have to keep her sedated and in intensive care for now. "

The pet rescue effort consisted of numerous unaffiliated animal groups that consolidated their efforts but remained relatively autonomous. The Pet Rescue Hotline, as it came to be called, was the top of the pyramid, and all available and relevant information was given to them. The welfare of the pets was foremost. No formal divisions of labor had been specified, but duplication of tasks was avoided, and the duties of one organization or group did not overlap those of the others. The Hotline, where people could call in and give descriptions of their missing pets, was in full operation by this time. Plans were made to have it staffed from 8 a.m. to 5 p.m.

Other wildfires across the West were overshadowed by the one in Oakland and Berkeley. In Los Padres National Forest a nineteen hundred-acre fire, the same size as the Northern California one, was beginning to be contained. Cool, moist air helped the firefighters there. Eastern Washington had lost over one hundred homes and had two deaths as fire blackened forty-three thousand acres near Spokane. In Idaho, four homes and several cabins were destroyed in the northern section of the state. One person died as a result. Firefighters fought a seventy-one-hundred-acre blaze in Wyoming. In Montana, fires burned over two hundred thousand acres in the Judith Mountains and in the Purcell Mountains. Three people were dead and seven homes were destroyed. Colder temperatures and rain and snow helped firefighters make significant progress on these fires. In the aggregate, the number of acres that had burned in these six western states far exceeded that which had burned in California, but the number of deaths and homes lost made the toll in California far surpass that of the other states combined. More people had died and more homes had been lost on one block in the Oakland/Berkeley fire than had been taken in six other states.

Doll Stanley went back to the fire zone that morning and managed to talk the police into letting her into the area to find animals. Although it was required that there must be an insignia on a vehicle in order to gain entry, Doll convinced them that she did belong to an animal organization and they allowed her in.

The first cat Doll trapped was not the cat that she was searching for that first day. She had gone to look for another cat and instead, trapped a Lynx Point Siamese male in the 400 block of Gravatt Drive. She was elated at this first capture!

On Tuesday afternoon, Stan Smith, who was staying at his brother-in-law's home in San Leandro, just south of Oakland, was dumbfounded when he returned to the house and heard the message on the answering machine. It was Berkeley Dog & Cat Hospital saying that they had Dudley. Stan raced to the veterinary hospital, expectant yet fearful of it all turning out to be a cruel error. He had been convinced Dudley had perished along with his wife.

He arrived at the hospital and the staff brought out the big dog. Dudley saw Stan and bounded over to him, despite his bandaged paws, yelping and crying, as if he were telling Stan the entire horrible story. Stan knelt on the floor and held the brave dog. He buried his face in Dudley's fur and wept.

Wednesday Morning, October 23, 1991

Esther Rasmussen's good friend and fellow Dane, Fritze, had watched the fire from her home in Sausalito, north of San Francisco. As the reports on Sunday had worsened, Fritze phoned Esther's relatives in Denmark to try to reach her. She did not have to break any bad news. Esther had already seen her home burn as she watched CNN. She had resigned herself to the loss, but was worried about her cat, Mr. Fox. Another friend of Esther's, Oscar, had been taking care of the house in her absence and had slipped back to the house the day of the fire. He was desperate to find Mr. Fox, but the orange and white tabby was not around. In the panic, as the fire bore down towards the house on Contra Costa Road, Oscar turned on all the faucets in a futile gesture to save the house. Ironically, Esther had just replaced the roof with the most fire retardant one available on the market, but it was of no use—it just took a little longer to burn.

Fritze and Oscar called Esther frequently. They all felt that since Mr. Fox spent a great deal of time outdoors he would probably not have been inside or would have left quickly. Because her property borders Lake Temescal Regional Park, Mr. Fox would have a relatively easy path of escape if he had not been overcome by the smoke. Although a lot of the area surrounding Lake Temescal had burned, it is nestled in a little valley and portions of it were spared when the fire leapt across the canyon. Perhaps Mr. Fox had sought refuge there. By the third day, Fritze had come up with a plan, which she shared with the other two. Mr. Fox would return if he heard familiar voices. When they could get up to the property, they should carry on conversations and let him know that they were still around. Esther was due to come back this week, but Fritze discouraged her. Why come back? There was nothing to come back to.

On Wednesday morning, Fritze and Oscar made the depressing journey up to see the destruction. They talked and talked while they walked around the property, hoping to lure Mr. Fox out of hiding. After a good fifteen minutes, Fritze had an idea. They could use a tape recorder to play their voices all night long. She telephoned Esther in Denmark. Esther heartily endorsed the idea, but why not play some of the classical music she always played while at home? That would fill in and give Mr. Fox something familiar to hear. Anything was worth a try.

As had so many others, Jan Jacot made the journey up to see the remains of her house, although she knew a few minutes after she fled that it was gone. She wanted to see if her cat, C.T., had survived. She had managed to rescue her other cat, but C.T. was nowhere to be found. The fire had started to surround her and there was no time to look for him. Like Norma Armon, Jan took food and water up with her when she went up under police escort to view her property. The barren landscape made her feel that there was only a slim chance C.T. had survived because the fire had been so thorough. Jan had heard that fish in ponds had survived, so she also brought along fish food to feed her fish and a net she borrowed from neighbors. Jan plunged the net into the sooty muck and found three of her four fish were alive. She was agog that they could have survived that long with so much slimy debris covering the surface of the water. She used the container of water she had brought as a temporary transport for them.

Jan dug around in the ashes and found a few recognizable items—some half melted silver dollars and a ceramic elephant that had belonged to her mother and that was blistered but otherwise undamaged.

The media had started to report about specific pets who had been found, and were printing the names of all the participating shelters, some of which were out of the area (one was in San Francisco).

As instructed by IDA, I was at the corner of College and Claremont Avenues at the appointed time, but the street coordinates I had been given were incorrect. I could not find the disaster relief center. I asked people on the street, but no one seemed to know where the building was. I could see and smell the burned hills and I was there to help, but where was the center? Finally, about the sixth person I asked knew what I was talking about and pointed me down the street. I had been told to go to the intersection of Claremont and College Avenues. The One-Stop Center was almost a mile further down Claremont Avenue, nowhere near that intersection, and was within a few hundred feet of the intersection with Telegraph Avenue. I wondered how many others had been given wrong directions and had just given up and gone home. Things were in a pandemonium for all involved, but basic information like this should have been given out correctly.

Outside, RVs were being used for insurance offices. Stepping inside, the Center was a beehive of activity. Everything had been thrown together hastily, but people seemed to be knowledgeable. It was difficult to tell who was a volunteer and who was a victim. Everyone looked the same. It made me realize that something like this could happen to anyone. These were ordinary people whose lives had been turned upside down. They no longer had houses to live in, but in spite of their shattered lives, they were maintaining their composures. I have never helped out in a disaster, and I did not know what to expect, but I did expect to be able to differentiate between the helpers and the "helpless."

I finally reached the table under the sign that said "Lost and Found Pets." It was the busiest table as far as I could see. Instead of the usual two people sitting at a table filling out a form as at the other tables, this table had at least a dozen people. I asked for Connie Cwynar, as I had been directed to do. Minutes later, a pretty, vivacious blond greeted me and gave me the run-through. What they needed immediately was for someone to go to a local market where, they had been told, people were placing Lost and Found advertisements about pets. Connie introduced me to another volunteer named Sue, and we set off to find the neighborhood grocery store. Sue told me on the way to the market that she had not lost her house, but had to evacuate. She had over an hour and a half to do so, and she helped her elderly neighbors prepare. When it came time to leave, she placed her two cockatiels in a brown paper bag, apologizing to them for the inconvenience. Their cage was much, much too large and would not fit in either car, so the bag was the only alternative. They did not mind, and when it was time to leave, her husband asked her what she had packed. "The only thing that matters to us," she told him, holding up the bag with the two birds. "You could at least have gotten us sweaters," he told her, running inside for one, as the police announced over megaphones to evacuate immediately. They did, leaving behind everything else in their lives. I liked her immediately

We copied ads for about an hour, one doing "Lost" and the other doing "Found." A young lady of about seventeen approached us and asked if we were with the Pet Rescue. Her mother, she told us, had just found a dog. We drove down the block and found her mother holding onto a large Golden Lab. I put him in the back seat and he looked relieved to have a soft spot to sit down on. Back at the center, I told them that I had not only copied the reports but I had even brought back a survivor. Everyone raced out to see the newest rescue.

After giving the dog food and water, the rescue volunteers scanned reports to see if he was listed missing. There were no reports that matched this dog, but that was not unlikely as many people had not been to the center yet. A "Found" report was filled out for the big dog and he had his picture taken to be placed in the book at the table inside. A foster home was arranged for him.

The survivors were coming to look at the pictures of the found pets, each brimming with anxiety and hope that their animal would be among them. Most were highly emotional, but still very much under control, until they faced the reality that their pet may not be found. They looked at the pictures, and read the found reports. Some were possibilities, but many did not match the descriptions. We tried to keep hope alive. "Keep coming to look at the pictures," we told them. "New animals are being found almost hourly."

Dorothy and Bob Sparks had driven down to their daughter's home after the fire, almost seventy miles to the south in Morgan Hill, California. They kept their motorhome stored there and decided to live there while they struggled to piece their lives back together. They bought a copy of the Oakland *Tribune* that day and eagerly read all the reports of the fire. In a small column labelled "Pets List," on the eleventh page of the main section they were dumbfounded when they saw among the ten cats listed, "Domestic short-hair, orange, male, neutered, tag reads 'Gus,' address 103 Starview, found at 45th and Broadway." Dorothy and Bob called the Oakland SPCA immediately and reclaimed Gus. They could not get back up to Oakland until the following day, but they knew that he was all right. He was not even on the injured cats list. Even more amazing was that Gus had traveled several miles that afternoon, transversing busy streets during the pandemonium when fleeing people were breaking all sorts of traffic rules. He was found within a block of the home of his previous owner who had passed away seven months before. Dorothy and Bob Sparks decided that Gus was obviously incredibly smart or very lucky. In any event, they were relieved to know that their little family was complete again.

The Sparks were lucky, too, in finding Gus. The rescue operation handled by Oakland was limited and disorganized. Besides Gus, the Pets List in the newspaper that day also included several cryptic and incomplete descriptions, often not even noting what kind of animal they'd located:

An orange and white long haired male, found at 7100 Westmoreland

A siamese adult, also found at 45th and Broadway

A black and white long-haired neutered male, at 720 Devon Way

A brownish-black long-haired, yellow eyes, tan flea collar found in the 6800 block of Broadway Terrace

A female Rottweiler mix, black and tan with white markings that had been found at Renwick and Brookdale.

A yellow lab, female. Unknown location.

Injured cats treated at the SPCA Clinic showed:

Two Siamese, one male, neutered.
Female Siamese/Seal Point
Burmese, male neutered
Domestic Black and white, medium hair, male.

In addition, one of the local papers had pictures of some of the cats. The black and white photos showed charred faces with crinkled whiskers, but no distinguishing features. The soot made all of the cats appear to be dark. Some of the animals just wanted to be left alone and did not pose well for the photographer.

The reports were beginning to mount up and several groups were combing the hills in an attempt to find disoriented stray animals. Concern was raised about the various shelters' policies regarding euthanizing animals after a certain time frame. Pets might be put down before the owners even had any idea where to look. Action had to be taken, and fast. Several groups proposed a moratorium on euthanization. The seventy-two hour limit for the Animal Shelter of Oakland, which was run by the police department, would have to be temporarily changed. It would be better to leave the animals running loose in the hills than to "rescue" them, only to kill them after three days. This was a disaster, extreme measures were necessary. Those of us involved with the Pet Rescue effort found it troublesome to deal with the bureaucracy of the city shelters. Valuable time was being wasted when so many more lost pets still had to be rescued.

Norma Armon with her daughter and son-in-law continued to search for Charmian. They looked at the photos and the descriptions in the papers, but could not locate the cat. Again, Norma made her pilgrimage up into the hills with Larry, the photographer. When she was at her property, she barely looked at the ruins other than to search for Charmian. Everything was gone, and she took on an almost detatched air about it. The one thing she clung to was hope that she would find "Charms." She continued to search everywhere she could, going twice a day to the shelters, but the cat had not been located. Norma dreaded the thought that her little friend was out there wandering around when she had been used to such a luxurious life. Norma had named her after Cleopatra's handmaiden, and treated her like royalty. Charmian was used to being outdoors, but always came home for her meals. It had been over three days. Some of the food had been eaten last night, but apparently by some other animal. If it had been Charms, she would have waited for Norma. Their bond was very strong. "A matter of time," Norma kept repeating to herself. "Just a matter of time."

Linda, Caryn Gottlieb's housemate, made it up to their house via a footpath that was unguarded. Miraculously, the house had survived, although Linda had been certain that it had burned shortly after she had left it on Sunday. The fire was coming directly at her when she loaded the cats into the truck and Zeb had made his own escape route through the forgotten open car window. The fickle wind had shifted and taken the flames along another path. Linda found the house intact, undamaged, although just four narrow lots away was utter destruction.

Caryn had told Linda her tale about the premonition of something terrible happening to Zeb. Caryn kept trying to focus on the additional part of the premonition: that whatever it was, Zeb would be all right.

On their front porch, Linda found a curiosity. The semi-circular plastic shade covering the porch light had been removed and set carefully against the wall and filled with water. Perhaps whoever had done that had seen Zeb and kindly left him water

Linda walked into the house and the phone began ringing. It was Caryn, calling from her Castro Valley office to see if the line had been redirected. She was shocked that someone had answered, especially Linda. "What are you doing there?" she asked incredulously. In the same tone, Linda replied, "Standing in the house. Its here! It was saved!"

While they were on the line, Zeb strolled into the room.

"Guess who's here?" Linda asked Caryn. After his first greeting to Linda, Zeb steadfastly refused to meow into the telephone receiver. Caryn rushed to the house as quickly as she could.

Zeb was very dirty and very hungry. There was no power at the house, so they could not remain there. They were not supposed to be there anyway, and the police had cordoned off the entire area. Caryn decided to take Zeb to her office for safekeeping. When they arrived and Caryn let Zeb out of the carrier, he dropped to the floor and crawled with his head down, like a soldier under fire. He would stop, raise his head up, darting it from side to side and then resume his crawling. Caryn and Linda reasoned that he must have been hiding under their house during the firestorm and for the two days afterwards. The noise level as the houses at the end of the block exploded and the abandoned vehicles on the street caught on fire must have been deafening. Cringing under his home, Zeb must have heard the helicopters and emergency vehicles nearby. He was perhaps the only living creature left in that neighborhood and he witnessed the firestorm from the front lines. His horror as the wall of flames approached him and then suddenly turned away as the wind shifted that afternoon is hard to imagine. Caryn's premonition had come true. She had known Zeb would be all right. He was.

Thursday, October 24, 1991

Beginning Thursday, October 24, the police barriers were removed and people were allowed to drive to their properties. The body of a sixty-four-year-old woman was discovered in the rubble of her home, bringing the death toll to twenty-four. There were still a number of people who were not accounted for and the death toll was expected to rise even higher.

It was rumored that workers near Buckingham Boulevard had begun the fire when they were either cooking lunch or burning trash, but the investigators were unable to substantiate the neighbors' reports. Seven people remained hospitalized, including an Oakland policeman in critical condition.

The churches and synagogues were holding services for the survivors. Everyone was coming to grips with the harsh reality and the magnitude of the loss. The One Stop Fire Emergency Center was now open with limited assistance, but would be fully operational within forty-eight hours.

The Berkeley Humane Society on Ninth Street in Berkeley donated a large space on the upper floor for the Pet Rescue Hotline. We were now operating full time and on weekends. Since Berkeley Humane Society is a non-kill shelter, they agreed to take as many pets as possible. Doll Stanley had bought all sorts of supplies, such as ropes in case it was necessary to descend down a cliff or to tie up a wayward dog, water buckets, and food. Doll first asked people that were congregated along the front lines if they had pets and where they had lived, thinking, perhaps naively, that the animals would just go home after the fire had ceased. She put out humane traps all over the hills and a small corps of volunteers was checking on them every few hours. Everyone felt relieved knowing that the pets could be kept safely at Berkeley Humane until they were claimed or placed in foster homes. It was the ones at the city shelters that had the volunteers worried.

Calls flooded the Hotline. Both lost and found reports were taken. The volunteers encouraged the survivors to look for their pets at all the shelters themselves, not to depend upon the Hotline to find the animal for them. Descriptions can vary greatly and only the person who knows the animal can actually identify it. Black cats, for example, all tend to have the same characteristics except for fur length. An orange cat might be referred to as "ginger," "buff," "beige," "red," "yellow," and "cream."

The volume of phone calls led the volunteers to believe that the number of animals that were lost far exceeded their original estimates. We all had assumed that people would have grabbed their pets first, but as the stories filtered in, it was clear there had been so little warning most people just didn't have time. Those that were able to find their pets often couldn't catch them. In the ensuing chaos of the day, the cats and dogs scattered and hid.

We at the Hotline knew that there would be busy weeks ahead. The trappers were beginning to tell about a few cats found in the middle of all the devastation. The ruins still smoldered but pets were sighted by neighbors and rescue crews returning to their properties. Not all life had perished in the eighteen hundred acres that had burned.

One of the search and rescue team members, John, thought he heard a cat cry as he was dishing out some food. Stopping and listening carefully, he heard nothing, and resumed his task. Then, he was certain he heard it again, and ever so slowly, so as not to scare away the frightened cat, he turned and surveyed the area around him, but saw nothing. He took a short walk around the property, softly calling and shaking the box of cat kibble, hoping to lure the cat out of its hiding place, but to no avail.

He returned to the exact spot where he had first heard the faint cry, and crouched down to listen. This time, he was sure he heard it. Perhaps the cat was trapped and could not come to him. Scouring the piles of ash and unrecognizable debris, he stopped every few feet to listen. The cry did not increase in volume, but now the cat responded feebly to his voice when he called out to it. Positive that there was a cat nearby, John persisted in his exploration of the area, limiting the radius of his investigation with each round.

He turned his attention to an area dominated by a large boulder. As he walked around it, the cry became more audible, and seemed to echo. Where the cry seemed to be the strongest, he got down on all fours and peered under the edge of the rock ledge. Using his flashlight, he found a crevice along one side of the rock. He squirmed under the tight projection and peered down into the darkness. Looking back at him were three tiny tabby kittens, no more than three weeks old. The cranny was about eighteen inches deep. Two of the kittens cried vociferously. The third tried, but had become too weak.

John carefully scooped the diminutive survivors to safety. Not having any kitten food, he minced up some canned tuna. The two stronger kittens needed no prompting to eat, but the third just stared at the dish. John tried putting a little bit of the juice from the tuna on the kitten's lips and it licked it off. He set it down, and it wobbled as it tried to stand, blinked, and approached the dish of food. Judging from their cautious eating style John realized that the kittens had not yet been weaned. After they finished their meal, John placed them in a carrier and returned to explore the crevice further.

The precipice ran jaggedly for a few feet, and at the opposite end from where he had found the kittens, John discovered the dead body of an adult female whose markings matched those of the kittens. In the midst of the firestorm, the mother cat had evidently carried each kitten to the haven of this crack in the ground, until she had been overcome by the smoke. For four long days, the kittens had been without nourishment and the comfort of their mother. They huddled, terrified, alone and helpless in the midst of a vaporized landscape until their rescuer arrived.

Jan Jacot again made the journey up to her home of eighteen years, or what remained of her home—the driveway and some melted lawn furniture. She called out at the top of her lungs for her cat, C.T. She was discouraged when she saw that the cat food she had left out the previous day had not been touched.

Other people were visiting their properties, picking here and there at the rubble that had been their lives. Two properties away, a woman called to Jan. "Are you looking for a kitty with a bell?"

"Yes!" Jan shouted back. She began to run towards the woman. She was beginning to shake all over.

The neighbor told Jan that they had moved aside a chunk of charred foundation wall about thirty minutes before, and a cat who had been hiding underneath it had scooted away, surprising them. Jan described C.T. to her, and the neighbor confirmed that the cat matched the description. She pointed out to Jan the direction in which the cat had run, and Jan retraced her steps back to the bottom of her own driveway.

Since everything around her was flattened, there was really no place for a cat to hide, and Jan scanned the area for any signs of the cat. She began to hear a faint "meow" in response to her calls, but could not find the source. Again and again she called, listening intensely for the slightest indication of where the cat was hiding. It was several minutes before Jan realized that the cat was in a small drainage culvert that runs under the foot of her driveway. "C.T.? C.T.? C.T.!" Jan called into the hole, which could not have been more than ten inches in diameter and was as long as the driveway is wide—over twelve feet. The cat inside responded with every call, but refused to emerge from its safe spot.

"Please, please, come to me," Jan coaxed, but the cat refused to budge.

Several interested neighbors gathered to help. The minutes stretched, and as they did so, Jan's anxiety rose.

Jan was positive that it was C.T. inside the culvert, but why would she refuse to exit the pipe? Surely she must recognize Jan's voice. Thirty minutes later, the small group of people still had not had any sort of success with dislodging the little hideout. Someone found an unburned length of pipe and began to gently prod the cat. After several more minutes of this, a very dishevelled and dirty C.T. scrambled out into the light and into Jan's arms. She had burned paw pads and singed ear tips and whiskers. Before Jan could rush C.T. away to the veterinarian's, the local Oakland television station had reporters and a camera crew that happened to be nearby and they taped the emotional reunion. That night, C.T. and Jan's story aired on the evening news.

Jan realized then how ultimately fortunate she had been. She had her family intact, and her own life had been spared. All around her was death and destruction. Jan vowed to rebuild her home and not to mourn the many material losses which she had suffered. Things could be replaced or remembered fondly. What mattered was that C.T. and Quadri were safe, and thanks to dear friends, the trio did not have to search for a place to live.

The cat which Karen Young had insisted her husband bring home with him early on Monday morning as he left the Montclair hillside had been brought into the SPCA for treatment as soon as they had opened on Monday. Karen had done what she could for the animal. She had nursed her thoughout the remainder of the night and felt triumphant that she had kept her alive. Now, four days later, the cat lay in the stainless steel cage, oblivious to the activity around her. Her picture had appeared in the newspaper, but no one had recognized her. She was listless and in pain, although the medicine was beginning to take effect and to ease the searing of her burns. Her feet were wrapped in dark pink bandages, making it difficult for her to walk or to stand. She was weak and made little effort to move around the small cage. The staff had nicknamed her "Smokey" and all wished that the little creature's family could find her. They were hopeful that it would speed her recovery. The numbers of injured animals increased every day as more and more were found by various groups who combed the hills looking for them. All too soon, the shelter was at capacity.

The number of people searching for their lost pets swelled as well, but there were not as many reunions as we had hoped for by this time. Among the crowd making the circuit of the four shelters in the two cities was Norma Armon. Everything else had become inconsequential to her. The main focus of her existence right now was to find Charmian. The photographer who had gotten her into the fire zone on his press credentials accompanied her as she made the rounds to all the places suggested by the Hotline. As they were inside the room housing the most severely injured animals, Norma turned to say something to Lloyd. Nearby, "Smokey" suddenly let out a loud "meow!" Norma rushed to the cage and dissolved in tears as she gripped the steel bars. Her distraught search had ended. Nothing else mattered to Norma at that moment, for she had found Charmian.

The staff explained that Charmian's picture had been in the newspaper. They showed Norma the article and photograph. Norma remembered seeing the picture, but the cat had in no way resembled Charmian. She felt terrible, knowing that she could have eased the pain for both of them if only she had recognized her in the newspaper.

Several residents of the Parkwoods Apartments gathered outside the entrance to the complex on Caldecott Lane. A temporary cyclone fence had been erected around the property and residents were forbidden access to it. The management claimed that it was for their own protection because of uneven debris levels and toxic wastes.

The apartment complex was among the nicest in Oakland. Situated near Highway 24, it offered luxury apartments and the usual range of amenities, such as a pool, sauna, workout rooms. But what made the apartments particularly appealing was the location of the complex. Parkwoods Apartments was nestled in a little valley in the hills that are otherwise occupied with single family residences. There was an extremely high occupancy rate among its 433 units. Because of the prevailing rent control laws, many people with various incomes could afford to live there. Among its residents were students, teachers, young professionals and retired people. There were seven three-story buildings that clustered around the swimming pool. Pets were allowed.

Sunday afternoon the fire swept down on the Parkwoods in a flash. It had begun just up the hill behind the complex, and Parkwoods was among the first and hardest hit of the residences. As the smoke bore down, the occupants tried to flee but discovered the electric gate would not open. The man in the first car, a Mercedes, crashed through the gate, freeing the other residents. When interviewed later, the man said that it was a dent that he would always be proud to have on his luxury automobile.

Members of the Contra Costa SPCA had congregated at the ruins of the complex and concentrated their rescue efforts there. Tamara Zinov was among the volunteers who had shown up early in the morning to help with the rescue. At first, they were denied access, but finally the management was persuaded to let them in to help find any surviving animals.

The only structures remaining were the concrete parking garages, which comprised the lower levels of all seven buildings. Integrated into them were laundry rooms, storage rooms, supply rooms and elevator shafts. The garages were vast and dark, littered with the charred remains of automobiles that had been ravaged by the inferno. Because of the extremely high temperature which the fire reached, there was a reasonable fear that the concrete had dried out, making it unsafe for anyone to be inside the structures. A cave-in of the concrete roof might happen at any moment.

A thorough search was made for human bodies among the wreckage. The firemen precariously looked inside each of the several hundred vehicles, but fortunately found no one. They reported to Tamara that they had heard a cat crying in one garage, but could not locate it. Whenever the firemen approached the group of vehicles where the crying seemed to be coming from, it ceased. Tamara cajoled the fire crew to let her enter and have a chance to rescue the cat. She promised them that she would do it as quickly as possible.

Tamara followed the plaintive cries until she came to a car from which the meowing emanated. She searched the vehicle, but there was no sign of a cat. Investigating further, she discovered that the cat was wedged deep into the upholstery of the back seat. Apparently there had been a rip in the covering and the cat had backed itself into the opening. The fire had raced through the car, scorching the seat covering, but it was extinguished rapidly. The thick layers of padding had insulated the hidden cat as the remainder of the car burned. The unfortunate creature had ensnared its rear paw in one of the metal springs of the car's upholstery and was trapped. Tamara freed the cat and carried him to safety. Outside, an anxious resident identified the cat as his own. Strangely enough, the car in which the cat had sought safety was in fact his owner's car.

Shortly after that, another volunteer from the Contra Costa SPCA, Pat Holmes, found a calico cat clinging to a board in a flooded elevator shaft. The cat had not made any noise, but on a routine search, her flashlight revealed the terrified animal, clinging for life in the pitch black chamber. It offered no resistance as she plucked it from its watery refuge. As the fire crews had attempted to save the complex, the shafts had filled with water where the cat had sought asylum, placing it in a predicament as life threatening as the one which forced it there.

Anxiously awaiting any word about her cat, Rebecca Foulkes kept a vigil outside the fence at the Parkwood site. Her two tabbies, year-old brothers named Tashi and Zephyr, had been locked inside her apartment. On Friday, Rebecca's heart leapt with unbridled joy when she saw Tamara carrying Zephyr to the gate. Zephyr gazed at Rebecca, touched her nose with his, then touched her mouth with his nose before seeming satisfied that it was in fact his Rebecca.

The Thursday Metro Edition of the *Oakland Tribune* carried a full page of updated listings of properties that were in the affected areas of the two cities. Alphabetically listed, it contained the names of streets. The explanation at the beginning claimed that the list might be inconsistent because street and house numbers have been obliterated. "OK" meant that the house or street was undamaged, damaged homes were noted as such, and "Gone" meant that the house was destroyed. Some of the notations were for complete streets or complete blocks. For example, "Gwin Way, gone," summed up the entire street. Streets such as Broadway Terrace, where the fire had hopscotched all over, took up half a column with each property getting a line. On some streets, such as Norfolk Road in Hiller Highlands, only one house was left standing. The saddest part was that the list was considered incomplete.

Friday, October 25, 1991

Rumors began to spread throughout the community that the main Animal Shelter on Ford Street in Oakland was killing pets to make room for animals coming into the facility from the fire zone and also that the incoming animals were being killed as well. Also circulating was the very disturbing rumor that animals were being killed in the fire zone by staff from the shelter, which is run by the Oakland Police Department. A senior animal control officer disputed the allegations, saying that only those animals already at the shelter and scheduled to be euthanized were being put down, that they were not doing so just to make additional room. They claimed that all pets brought in would be kept for a "reasonable amount of time" before being killed. The animal groups who were working independently of the shelter again called for a moratorium on euthanization. Time was what the animals needed.

The shelter admitted to euthanizing one animal, a cat who had been brought in so badly burned that there was no other alternative. It had been found with another cat who was licking its wounds in a futile attempt to save it. The shelter agreed to remain open until nine o'clock on Friday evening and until four o'clock on Saturday afternoon. However, in the midst of this disaster, they were going to be closed both Sunday and Monday. The officials at the shelter claimed that although hundreds of pets were reported missing, less than one hundred had been found and not many were still running loose. They declared that there were no more animals in the fire zone. The independent animal volunteers knew differently. Reports came in every hour expanding the missing pets numbers almost exponentially. The animals being found by the independent trappers increased every day as the cats and dogs and rabbits and tortoises came out of hiding. Five days is nothing after such a disaster.

Doll Stanley, continued to comb the hills eighteen hours a day, and always had evidence of food being eaten at feeding stations and usually had a cat in a trap every time she checked. Her eyewitness account of the first few days proved that there were many more animals up in those hills than previously estimated. Of the three thousand homes that were destroyed, many had pets. Most had multiple pets, so a very conservative estimate would be around five thousand animals. If only ten percent survived, that brought the total up to five hundred.

Not all of the animals stayed within the boundaries of the fire zone. They ran into the adjacent neighborhoods, and waited until the fire was out before returning. Five days later, the more skeptical among them might just be setting out for home.

The shelter officially withdrew from the search for any more animals. All of us engaged in the rescue effort were relieved. Now, those who would not kill the animals after only a brief period of time would have more control over the situation. Any pets found would be in the safest hands possible. Although there were still fire animals at the main pound, the euthanization process was being delayed. No one was certain what the "reasonable amount of time" was going to be, and the various groups banded together even more than they already were to press the police department to give them a concrete answer and date. Offers were made to take control and custody of the animals by the various groups, but they were refused.

At the Pet Rescue table in the One Stop Center, more than two hundred people had come in during the first five days of operation. One of the first to come to look at the pictures of the rescued pets was Paul Bentz. He scrutinized each photograph on the slim chance that it might be one of his cats, Nikki or Webber. He described their characteristics to us: Webber was a big, solid black cat who had escaped from his wife's grasp as she had attempted to put him in their car Sunday afternoon. In his frenzy, Webber had gotten away from Sarah, who, in the latter stages of pregnancy, was not in top form to wrestle with the strong cat. Nikki, on the other hand, had highly identifiable markings, according to Paul. He was a brown and black tabby with distinctive bull's-eye markings on his sides. He also had ear tufts which made him look like a bobcat. After a fruitless search of the photographs, which included the newspaper photos where Charmian's picture had appeared, Paul left to visit the shelters again.

Most people were too stunned to remember details about their pets, or could remember tiny idiosyncratic traits and not the general information. They filled out forms about their lost pets, which would be copied and brought over to the Hotline office at Berkeley Humane Society. Having to dwell on a pet's characteristics for the reports reinforced the fear that the animal may not have survived. People who had been stoic and solid and realistic throughout the rest of the process at the Center crumbled when filling out a lost pet report. Most had no hope, but we tried to instill it in them anyway. We were receiving frequent reports of animals being found alive and relatively unharmed. The volunteers tried to express to the survivors that anything was possible, but it was difficult to try to get someone to believe that their dog or cat could have survived the inferno.

One couple in their sixties stand out in my memory as perfect examples of the survivors' attitudes. Both the husband and wife were gracious, well-educated and accepting that what had occurred had been an act of nature that they could have in no way prevented. It did not matter what sort of material their roof was made of, it had gone up in flames as had everything else. They had been away that afternoon, leaving long before the brush fire rekindled. Their houseful of memories had all been incinerated, yet they were calm and rational. They came to report their cat, Babe, as missing. He was fifteen, pure white and had two teeth left. He had been locked inside their family room and the car underneath him in the garage had exploded. There had been a window open, and, this couple reasoned, if Babe had just clawed through the screen, he would have been outside. It was a twenty-five foot drop to the ground, however. The couple didn't really harbor much hope that the elderly cat had survived, but still they filled out a lost report and searched the found files, just in case there had been a miracle. They had had him since he was a kitten and could cope with the fact that he might be dead; however, just like everyone else, they wanted to know.

We went off to a private room to look at the found reports, but there was not one that matched their cat. I told them how it was still early in the rescue and how we were locating missing animals daily. Although it did not look good for their cat, I urged them not to give up the search.

The wife asked me if Babe would have suffered. I told her what my veterinarian had told me the previous day. The smoke inhalation would have made the animal faint first before the flames reached it. I told her that he would have been dead before the flames took over. She seemed relieved. If he had died, at least he had not been burned alive. They left with a sense of calmness.

Filing a report with the Hotline or at the One Stop Center seemed to give people hope. The mere act of placing their pet's characteristics on paper and knowing that someone was looking for them was reassuring. Most everyone who came to search felt that the animal was a part of the family. The important thing was to have a report on file. Already pets had been found who did not have reports that matched, but it was only six days after the fire. In the weeks to come, the volunteer groups were positive that there would be no animals left unclaimed. We believed it was all a matter of time until the singed and sooty were reunited with their loved ones.

I got a firsthand look at the devastation that afternoon. I met Doll Stanley at the corner right below the Claremont Hotel. Standing there, we could still smell the burned remnants as the wind wafted downhill. We went up around the hotel. I followed her in my car, loaded with the supplies that I had been asked to bring: canned tuna for cats, hot dogs for the dogs, bottles of water, plastic bowls, dry kibble for both kinds of animals, a flashlight, some boots and heavy gloves. Immediately behind the hotel, we climbed a very steep, short street. There was lots of vegetation, mature trees, and homes that were intact and looked to be miles from any disaster. I wondered when we were going to be in the fire zone and before I could finish the thought, we made a curve left and before me was nothing but a monochromatic moonscape. It was all black and gray with charred stumps that had been lofty trees. There were chimneys and fireplaces standing erect each marking a home. A few outside stairs remained, leading to non-existent homes.

Doll pulled into a cul-de-sac that had been partially ravaged. At one home left standing, she knocked on the door. She had to get this report before we went further. The woman who answered was gracious but frazzled. Yes, they had found a black and white cat on the back of their property, but it was dead and half burned. They had buried it and she attempted to give us a description of it, but couldn't remember many details, including the sex. She excused herself to return to the straightening of her home. Although it was intact, the damage had been heavy. Windows had blown out, the roof had been partially burned and all of the contents smelled of smoke. There were no utilities yet, so any work that could be done had to be done in the waning autumn light. They had to remove any valuables, since there had been reports of looting. We went back to the cars. On the way we found a lizard that had perished in the fire. Doll gently picked it up and went over to a secluded part of an adjacent property and buried it.

A couple of turns and we were in the thick of it. All around were undulating hills of ash, punctuated by on occasional chunk of something unrecognizable. The streets were lined with burned-out hulks of automobiles. Some had been marked with yellow spray paint by insurance companies, thus identifying them by their make and license number. It was difficult to tell what kind of a car each charred piece had been.

We were flagged down by a worker along Amito Road. He told us that there was a cat in one of the traps that Doll had set out and was closely monitoring. We found a big unhappy black and white male cat. He had come for the tuna. Doll spoke to him in a reassuring voice, trying to calm him down. Next she took two pictures of him with a Polaroid camera. Doll explained that although using a Polaroid was more expensive, we could tell instantly if the picture were usable or not. She wrote the date and location on the finished pictures. One was for the photo books at the One Stop Center, the second was for the Hotline. The proverb about a picture being worth a thousand words rang true here. There was no point in launching into a lengthy description of a pet—this way the viewers of the photo books could see for themselves if the animal looked or did not look like their lost animal.

Doll and I transferred the cat into a carrier and placed it in the rear of her small pickup truck. Again she replaced the food and water in the trap and reset the door.

She told me about how many animals she had found and how many were still in these hills. After a half hour or so, Doll gave me my instructions. "Just place the food in a safe spot. Pick whatever looks right to you," she told me before making her departure. "There's really no right or wrong way to do this. There are vast open spaces and these animals need to be fed, whether we eventually capture them or not. Make a list of where you left the food so you can check on it the next time you go around. If you see a trap that's got a cat or dog, just bring in the whole thing to Berkeley Humane." With a warm smile, she was gone. I stood looking at the devastation before me and started leaving out food. It was difficult to mark down exactly where I had left it, as there were no addresses and no house numbers. A few street signs survived that at least gave me a name to go on, but most were twisted to the ground or utterly obliterated. When I did not have a name, I looked around and tried to memorize the spot. Sometimes there was a little telltale sign that helped me. One time it was a chunk of a pink stucco wall. I wrote it down on my list and noted that the food was to the right of the stairs. The piece of pink stucco wall could have fit into the trunk of my car, but I could not find another thing on that property that was recognizable.

After seeing so much devastation, I was practically sick to my stomach. Around every curve was just more of the same—ashes. I was alone up there on that October afternoon, but for a few birds that flitted among the gnarled, charred branches of the handful of trees that remained. I did not see any other animals, but decided that if there were birds, any cats in the area might be attracted to them. At least some wildlife had chosen to return. That was a good sign.

I continued driving along Grandview Drive and as I rounded the curve near Dorothy Place, the panorama of destruction that I beheld literally stopped me in my tracks. I had been in the ruins for over two hours, and thought that I had seen most of it, but the vista before me was astounding. So far, I had seen only a tiny portion of the destruction. It was incredible. I stopped and got out of the car. The feeling of grief at the tremendous loss held me immobile, standing and staring at the hillsides covered with nothing but ashes and chimneys.

As soon as they were allowed back onto their property, the Dobson family spent hours trying to find their missing cats. They knew that the cats, if they were within hearing distance, would respond to the familiar sounds of their voices, so the family spent every evening at their lot, loudly carrying on a conversation. They sat in lawn chairs throughout the now chilly October nights, attempting to coax their four cats, Tao, MaMa, Mimi, and Skids back to them. Tralee Dobson knew that the entire process might take a while. She had lost a Siamese when she was a teenager. Five years later, an identical cat appeared, and Tralee would not have believed it was her cat until she discovered an identifiable scar on its leg. A week was nothing, no real time at all. It became a focus, a goal for the family to find their cats. By the first weekend, they decided to camp out at their lot and brought provisions for an overnight stay. Their house had been situated on Caldwell Road, near Highway 13. They had had some warning, but the cats were not around during their evacuation. Sixteen-year-old Courtney Dobson had taken her photo album and almost nothing else. When she filled out the lost forms at the One Stop Center, she was able to give a very detailed description of her cats, and to supply the Hotline with color copies of the pictures.

Doll Stanley spent so much time every day in the hills that the crews searching for human victims came to know her and flagged her down if they had seen an animal. It was a network that became invaluable to Doll. She was up in the hills at two or three in the morning, making sure that if any animal were found in a trap it would not be exposed to the elements for too long. It might also be injured and need veterinary attention. Some animals will go berserk when enclosed and Doll did not want any of them to harm themselves.

As an employee of In Defense of Animals, it was determined that Doll should continue her work in the fire zone for one month.

The volume of volunteers for all of the fire-related assistance was overwhelming. There was indeed, a surplus of people who would give their time and expect nothing in return. The community of the San Francisco Bay Area really showed its generosity, not just in financial terms, but also in time. Many businesses donated their goods and services. Many discounts were available to the survivors. Even large-ticket items such as automobiles were offered at special rates from local dealerships to those who had lost theirs. A national linen warehouse donated new bedding to a large number of the fire survivors who had moved into an apartment complex. The "refugee" centers were closing, but some of the food that was served there was from the top notch four star restaurants of Berkeley and Oakland.

The media was giving the pet rescue effort a lot of attention. It let people know that the animals were still being found and that everyone should file a report and not give up searching.

Sunday, October 27, 1991

"I got out with my life, but I had to leave my best friend behind. Now I want him back," said one of the fire survivors, who was quoted in the local newspaper on this date. It succinctly summed up the feeling of hundreds of people. The writer, Gary Bogue, stressed that he had been on both sides of animal rescues for many years. He questioned the response from the city Animal Shelter, which insisted all surviving animals had been found, and how those officials tried to prevent the private animal groups from participating in the searches. Gary's point that day was: if pets are still alive in the area, we must find them—together.

It was a strong message that cut across the lines that had been drawn. There was no sense in any political battling. There were animal lives at stake and they needed to be saved.

One of the most important aspects of the coordinated rescue effort was the photographing of the found pets. Ellie Hoffmann, a professional photographer in Berkeley, realized that it would be the best way to help identify the animals. The photo books were at the One Stop Center. People could come and see the pictures instead of traipsing around to the various shelters and foster homes. Many pets had been reported but not photographed yet, so a volunteer band, which included Doll Stanley, set out to acquire photos of all the found animals. This way, the traumatized animal would be minimally disturbed, and the survivors could make a stop by the table to see the pictures. It also spared people from having to view wounded and suffering animals. The photo books acted as a buffer, although some of the pictures were still painful to see. The injured faces had to be shown in order for the owners to recognize their pets. Most people faced the task with resignation, understanding that these injuries were to be expected after such a disaster.

Dead animals, if they were not burned beyond recognition, were also photographed, but warnings were given to people before they looked at these pictures, which, in fact were very few. Everyone coming to search for their pets wanted an answer, and though gruesome, such a photo would provide one for someone. It would allow them to grieve and go on with their lives and they could quit wondering what had become of their friend.

The "Lost and Found Pets" sign was up at the rear of the One Stop Center. It was staffed mainly by those who were associated with In Defense of Animals. A sizable group of volunteers had been called upon from their ranks. Others, like myself, who had volunteered to assist with the project were associated with other groups or were there individually.

One of the first people I met there was Yvette Resnick. Outgoing, personable, and quick to learn, Yvette had been a realtor in the area for a couple of decades and knew the burned area very well. Her knowledge of almost every street proved to be invaluable during the first few weeks. She also knew a lot of the people who came to look for their pets, some having been clients of hers in the past.

Yvette applied her "people" skills to the situation. She greeted everyone, explained our process, and guided them through it. A number of "animal people" did not possess such talents, and tended to forget the human factor. There was nothing wrong with this, but they just were not that good in dealing with people in the first place, and distraught, emotional survivors of a natural disaster were beyond their ken.

After two or three times staffing at the table, Connie Cwynar took me aside and asked me to please help out on a regular basis. I was working the "front lines," so to speak, but it was the dedicated work of so many behind the lines that made my work possible.

Kathryn Howell, an actress, had watched the fire from her home in Oakland that Sunday and marked off the streets as they were announced on the news broadcasts. It was a full week before she could locate the Pet Rescue operation that was not related to the city shelter. On her first day, Kathryn walked into the Hotline office at Berkeley Humane Society on Ninth Street and into a beehive of activity.

Another of the Hotline volunteers was Rose Lernberg. Her superb organizational skills were a major contribution to the Hotline. Involved for more years than she can remember in animal causes, Rose was among the first called upon by Patt Shaw to help coordinate the paperwork and the telephone duties. Rose's steel-trap memory and her eye for intricate detail helped enormously during the first tumultuous days as the entire plan became effective.

There were no former rescue efforts to look to for assistance. This was the first time a large-scale rescue of companion animals was taking place. The recent Loma Prieta Earthquake of October 1989, had displaced a lot of animals over a wide area. Many animals returned to their homes or neighborhoods within a reasonable time period after the quake. This was not possible in Oakland—the neighborhoods were simply gone.

There have been other organized animal rescue efforts that preceded the Oakland Fire, but these involved wildlife. An oil spill in San Francisco Bay, for example, resulted in thousands of sea birds and marine life needing attention. The firestorm did affect a lot of wildlife, but it was especially devastating to domestic animals who had no way to fend for themselves. They were utterly dependent upon their human companions.

Diane McDermott was actively involved in the Pet Rescue just hours after returning from her European vacation. As a very active member of IDA she had learned about the disaster while still overseas and had barely slept when she showed up to help out.

Judith Cwynar, Connie's sister, donated her time to help enter computer data about the various pets and also shuttled the photographs from the photographers to the One Stop and to the Hotline.

Each person's contribution was an integral part of the rescue. Combined with the efforts of various groups, such as East Bay Animal Referral (EBAR), the effectiveness of the entire operation was being maximized. There was little or no squabbling. Everyone was focused enough on the important issue of rescuing animals to put any personal differences aside and get the work done.

Tuesday, October 29, 1991

Since the fire, Norma and her daughter, Carla, and son-in-law, Jon, had been staying at their business offices in Oakland. Norma Armon was allowed to take Charmian with her, but only for a few hours.

The three of them felt renewed because of having found Charmian. Now the frantic days of worrying and searching were over and life could resume as best as possible.

Norma played Charmian's favorite classical music, Mozart's Horn Concerto and Brahm's Violin Concerto in an effort to make everything as normal as possible for the severely injured cat. Charmian was very quiet and only meowed when in pain. She had been quite a talker before the fire, but now she lay silently looking at Norma.

Norma did all she could think of to help Charmian back on her path to recovery. She felt so encouraged when Charmain ate some canteloupe, her favorite food. She doted on the little cat, talking to her and telling her how horrible that day had been, not being able to find her and how she had left every door and window and cabinet open so Charmian could escape. Norma gingerly stroked Charmian and looked into her eyes. Now their lives could go on. All the rest of it, the house and all that was incinerated, seemed so unimportant. Norma was certain that this little visit would bolster Charmian's spirits and help her to heal.

Kelli Smith and her mother and stepfather, Terri and Rod Hensley, had no hope of ever finding Max, the big black and white cat who had hidden under her bed as Kelli fled their Hiller Highlands townhouse. Up at the lot, they attempted to search for any signs of him, but rubble was strewn everywhere. As the townhouses exploded, their contents had mingled together. The Hensleys found pieces of items that they did not recognize. Their next-door neighbor found shards of the Hensley's china within the perimeters of her foundation. The family felt awful that Max could not have been rescued, but considering that Kelli had barely escaped with her own life, they were certain that she would have perished if she had remained in the house trying to save the cat. Kelli felt especially bad since Max had scooted right past her as she went upstairs. She had been so certain that the fire department would save the townhouse and that Max would be all right. Kelli's sister, Kathy, had come down from college in Oregon to be with the family during this crisis period. She had insisted that they look for Max, although he was Kelli's cat and not hers. Kathy encouraged her family to fill out a report with the Hotline and to search all the shelters. It was a valiant effort, although Rod and Terri felt that it was absolutely hopeless. They would go with their daughters on the search if it made them feel better, but considering the circumstances, there was not a shred of evidence that Max could have survived the explosion. He had been locked indoors, and every window had been securely shut by Kelli in her attempt to keep out the smoke. Hiller Highlands had been in the worst part of the fire. Most of the human deaths had happened right in their own neighborhood. A young woman, not much older than Kelli had perished while she waited for someone to come and save her. The 911 dispatcher told her that someone would definitely come by and get her out. No one did. The more that Rod and Terri Hensley heard about the tradgedies that had occurred so close to their home, the more blessed they felt. It was terrible about Max, but a few seconds or a minute might have turned into an even greater tragedy for the family.

Kathy was the only one to keep the hope alive that Max might be found. Her optimism buoyed the family through the aftermath of the disaster. "Just let's look again," she told them. In an attempt to keep focused, they once again visited the animal shelters, and once again, were disappointed.

The response from the public in reporting found animals was far greater than we had expected. The Oakland Animal Shelter's spokesperson stated in a newspaper article that their own search teams that numbered only up to ten people per day in the nineteen-hundred-acre area were finding only three live animals and almost three times as many dead ones. They claimed in the media that they were not really "finding that many animals alive up there, although there are sightings of cats running around." Shortly after, just a week after the fire, they ceased their search altogether.

A "sighting" was when someone saw an animal that they could not capture. Although it may sound on the surface to be a fruitless endeavor, sightings nevertheless gave an indication of animal survival. A sighting also gave a possible match up to a pet on a lost report that had been filed. Although the sighting may be no more than a passing glance, a report of a certain marked cat in the radius of its former home might indicate that the cat was on its way back or had decided to remain in a particular area where it felt safer. To hear about a cat that looked like yours and was just down the hill from where you had lived would give you a lot of hope, and hope was what people needed.

The survivors themselves were strongly encouraged to participate in the search and rescue of their own pets The area was three square miles, and even if the rescue feeders and trappers were increased ten-fold, it still probably would not have been enough manpower to effectively cover the fire zone. A number of cats, such as Jan Jacot's C.T., had stayed near the house during the firestorm. Of course, C.T., may have fled and returned immediately. We will never know, but considering that she was hiding in a drainpipe, it is most likely the area where she sat out the conflagration. She felt safe there and ran to it again when confronted with danger.

The survivors would know their pets and perhaps their neighbor's pets and could identify them on sight. A rescuer might have a report of a certain pet having lived at a certain address, but could not be positive about any other animal in the immediate area.

Because of the spread-out proportions of the fire zone, it would be impossible to leave food out at every location where a pet had been reported missing, so food and water were left where animals could get to them easily.

Canned tuna was recommended for the cats and hot dogs for the dogs. Dry kibble of both varieties was left as well. The choice of tuna was not just that most cats liked its flavor; the strong scent carried farther than other choices and thus stood a better chance of attracting cats that were not in the immediate area.

The dry kibble served two purposes: it fed the domestic animals and the wildlife, such as raccoons, as well. This week, hay bales were scattered throughout the area for the deer.

The homeowners were asked to be on the lookout for any animals while they were up at their properties and to report them to us as soon as possible. The human survivors would be in more locations than the rescuers, who were now mainly working in solitary fashion. The survivors would also be sifting through the remains of the properties and might discover pets' hiding places.

It became more apparent that animals were up in the zone in larger numbers than previously suspected. Cats, especially, were appearing due to an intricate network of culverts and drains that honeycombed the hillsides. They had taken refuge in these systems during the fire, and feeling safer there left only to forage for food.

There is no doubt that hundreds of animals perished that day and immediately afterwards, but so many of them had escape routes and took them, some, like Dorothy's Gus, leaving before their human companions were aware of the fire.

Because of the rumors circulating in the community about animals being euthanized after only a few days of being at the shelters, some people who had found pets refused to turn them in or to even report them. On more than one occasion the Hotline got a very reluctant anonymous call and had to reassure the finder that the animal was in no danger of being taken away from them and killed. It was necessary for us to explain again and again that this rescue effort was independent of the Oakland Animal Shelter's short-term project.

Dogs and cats comprised the majority of the finds, but turtles, tortoises, rabbits, and birds were also found. One woman called to say that two pheasants flew into her yard on the afternoon of the fire. Her home was within reasonable proximity of the fire, so it seemed likely the birds had fled the approaching flames. The woman said that they were tame, and she could care for them. Ducks, geese, parrots, cockatiels, parakeets, and canaries also were reported. In the melee that day, some people had no other choice but to release their pet birds, thereby giving them a chance to escape.

The variety of animals and the sheer numbers were mounting higher. Not all were injured or even singed, but all were traumatized.

Wildlife was returning to the area. At the Parkwoods Apartments near the site of the beginning of the fire, the management had the entire property fenced off. Three stories of apartments had collapsed, mingling whatever things might have survived the inferno. The residents were angry that they were not allowed access, especially when the rents had been paid through the end of the month, but the management was concerned about the possible injuries to tenants searching through the rubble.

While the chain-link fencing was being placed around the large property, deer had wandered into the area. The fire had ceased at Grizly Peak Boulevard, not too far to the east and uphill from the complex. Animal Control Officers had monitored the section and discovered a fawn.

They observed it for some days, and it looked well nourished and they assumed that the mother was still alive and caring for it, although they had not seen the doe. When the management of the Parkwoods enclosed the property, the fawn was inside it. The animal panicked and leaped and dashed about desperately trying to find an exit, but it could not. It repeatedly threw itself against the fencing to try to get back to its mother. It died, apparently of a heart attack, during its futile attempt at freedom.

There were reports of animals who returned to the site of their homes on their own. One couple was surveying the remains of their home when they were found by their two dogs, whom they believed had perished. The dogs cautiously approached the couple, with tails wagging but with guilty looks on their faces as though they feared the fire was somehow their own fault. It took some coaxing and reassuring words from the joyful owners to bring the dogs around to their normal bouncing demeanors.

Many cats began to return under their own volition as well. The Hotline began to receive reports from owners who notified us that while on a visit back to the property their cat was waiting for them, acting as if nothing had happened. It was encouraging news that we as volunteers could relay to those who were still desperately searching for their own lost pets.

Fritze and Oscar kept checking Esther Rasmussen's lot for any signs of her cat, Mr. Fox. They were encouraged when they found that again the food they had left out had been eaten. Fritz knew it would soften the blow of the loss of the home and its contents if Esther could have Mr. Fox back. Esther was due to return to the states soon.

Two nights before Esther was due back, Fritze and Oscar went to the property early in the morning. Walking up the driveway, the singing of Luciano Pavarotti from the tape recorder that they had placed there filled the cool gray morning air. With great anticipation, Fritze and Oscar saw that the food had been eaten. They peered inside the box they had left for the cat, and there was Mr. Fox, curled up asleep! The great performer had lured the cat home. Mr. Fox, the cat who loved Pavarotti, dreamily opened one eye and snuggled down into the towel.

As soon as she could reach her home across the Bay, Fritze called Esther with the good news. Esther had suspected all along that Mr. Fox would survive. She thought of the cat that had been locked in her car and how she was unsure what sort of a sign Mr. Fox had sent to her.

Eight days after the fire, a crew who was restoring electrical utility lines near Broadway Terrace found a seriously injured black and white cat and took it to the SPCA shelter on Hegenberger Road. The next day, Kelli Smith's sister, Kathy, insisted on a final search for Max at the various shelters before she returned to college in Oregon. Terri, in an attempt to placate her daughters, accompanied Kathy, although she still felt that it was a futile gesture. After all, Max had been locked inside their townhouse when it exploded.

At the SPCA, they found a bandaged cat whose whiskers had been burned off, as had part of his ear and the fur on his tail. All of his paw pads had been almost totally burned off. He was bandaged and was being fed intravenously. Kathy and her mother summoned a staff member to ask what information was on the ID tag on the cat's collar. They were amazed to discover that the cat was, in fact, Max. Kathy and Terri immediately called Kelli with the good news. When she arrived and the attendant opened the cage, Max roused himself from his drug-induced stupor and gave Kelli and long, familiar look, obviously recognizing her. Then he blinked and went back to sleep.

After the townhouse exploded, Max had arduously traveled almost three miles to the site of the family's former home, where they had lived up until six weeks before the fire. Their former house had also burned and the thunderous sounds of the repair crew with their heavy equipment must have been terribly frightening, yet he stayed close by. Instinctively, Max had known precisely where to go, although he had never actually walked the distance before. He also knew that this specific pile of debris had once been his home. Max must have decided that his family would eventually come for him. As severely injured as he was, his determination to find his family led him on a truly incredible journey.

Some people seemed to give up rather easily, even when the animal had the best chances of survival. Many pets were being found that were obviously survivors of the fire, but were unclaimed. It was hard to imagine that these pets had a loving home until October twentieth, only to be forgotten or presumed dead. Rescue workers had expected that within two weeks eighty percent of the animals would be positively idenitifed and claimed by their owners. Foster care was available for those who could not keep their pets at the present time.

The longer we could keep the operation going, the more pets would be claimed, we figured. It was still very soon after the disaster and as the shock wore off for some people, and they became aware of our operation, we would be able to instigate more reunions of lost pets with their families.

Wednesday, October 30, 1991

Norma delivered Charmian back to the veterinarian's office, and went home to wait until the hospital called for her to come and pick her up again. Charmian had shown some progress, but remained very subdued. The cat's recovery had become Norma's focus, and the only thing that she and her family now cared about.

When the telephone rang that afternoon, Norma expected it to be the clinic telling her what time she should pick up Charmian. Instead, the vet was calling to say that Charmian had died. Norma had been so certain that Charmian had been getting better. She was devastated.

The next day, the family buried Charmian in a deserted foxhole far up the side of a barren, burned hill overlooking one of the paths where they had taken so many walks together.

A few days after Charmian's passing, Norma had a dream that comforted her. In it, Charms was not the singed and quiet cat that she had been since the fire, but was rather her former self—fluffy and attentive. She seemed serene and happy. Norma believes that the dream was a message urging her to cease dwelling on all that the fire took from her. She has done exactly that, although she will never forget the wonderful years that she and Charmian shared.

Frequently, people would be confused when looking at the pictures of the found animals. The volunteers had to stress that imagination was necessary, that the dog or cat may not look like its former self. Some people just flipped quickly through the pages. One of the obviously black cats had been labelled as "becoming orange." The amount of soot on its coat had radically changed its appearance to the point where the coat color was not even certain. It had been bathed, but its color changed to a lighter shade as the days progressed. We informed the people searching for their pets of this discrepancy and urged them to go look at any cat that even vaguely resembled their own.

Many of the animals were traumatized and did not pose easily for pictures. Sometimes they would have to be held still and someone's hand might resemble a marking. We had to make specific notes on certain pictures to let people know that what might appear to be a white or light-colored bib on a cat was, in fact, someone's fingers.

One couple particularly stands out in my memory. The wife, seated at the table and looking through the photo books found a picture of what she believed to be her cat. The husband, standing behind her, merely glanced at the picture, said "no," and turned away, rocking back and forth on his heels, obviously anxious to leave. The wife insisted that it looked like their cat, but the husband, his temper growing short, said it did not. The picture was a photocopy of a newspaper and was not a good shot to begin with, but apparently the best that the photographer could accomplish under the circumstances. An original had not yet been acquired for our photo books. The cat in question was singed, its whiskers crinkled stubs. Added to everything else, it was a brown, black, and gray tabby, with no unusual markings. The couple was obviously under enormous strain, but they had taken the time to search for their cat. For whatever reasons, they were in conflict. I stressed to the wife that they should go and look, "just to make sure," because the cat may have radically changed in appearance due to injuries. The husband, who may not have liked the cat to begin with, or who was too afraid to delve deeper for fear of emotional upheaval, chose to write off this possibility altogether.

Sometimes confusion arose over the terms "lost" and "found." A nearby bulletin board held pictures and written pleas about specific pets that people were searching for. The photo books were of the pets that had been found. Some people needed guidance and specific instructions on even the most basic phases of the rescue. This illustrated to us just how deeply the disaster had affected them.

I began to put in more hours dealing with those who were looking at the photo books. I also tried to get up into the fire zone to leave out food and water, but considering the fifty miles between my home and Oakland, it was not always possible to do so.

Daylight Savings Time was ending, making it dark by about five o'clock. It was a hindrance and an annoyance for most of the searchers, except for Doll Stanley and John LaMott, who joined our efforts. The two rescuers, through sheer dedication, spent nearly every night searching the narrow deserted streets and checking the traps. Animals tend to feed at dawn and dusk, so those were the best times to be up in the hills. Working separately, John and Doll and the others frequently encountered each other in the vast, eerie darkness, startling each other as their paths overlapped. John, a tall, handsome bearded man, worked and went to school in addition to helping with the rescue effort at night.

One of the newspaper delivery people rescued three cats and a dog in the first ten days following the fire. One day while I was up in the zone, I came across the mail delivery person and asked her to keep an eye out for stray pets. Even though there were no homes to deliver mail to, service was in place, and some mail was delivered in the few remaining, twisted mailboxes. It seems that they do live up to their motto. Even the obliteration of the residences did not deter the U.S. Postal Service.

October turned into November and no one seemed sentimental to see it leave. A local newspaper columnist remarked that October, although usually one of the prettiest months in California, should officially be banned from our calendars, since we had had two huge disasters in that month within two years: the Loma Prieta Earthquake in 1989, and now the Firestorm of 1991.

The chunk in the foreground is all that remains of a car.

Stan Smith and Dudley.

Diana Ragen with Kacie Ragen and Pumpkin.

Noreen Cardinale and Sammy were reunited on the second anniversary of the firestorm. (PHOTO BY MIKE FITELSON)

Eric Gilliland and Katrina.
(PHOTO BY MIKE FITELSON)

Mr. Fox and Pavarotti. (PHOTO BY SVEND SCHJOERRING)

Caryn Gottlieb (left) and Linda with Zeb (orange), Sasha, and Keeper.

George Perko (left) and Phil Stanley with Marduk.

Jay Stewart and Chad.

Kelli Smith and Max. Max was blown out of the Hiller Highlands townhouse.

Gus Sparks. (PHOTO BY DOROTHY SPARKS)

Two-year-old Scott O'Connell and Blackie. Blackie was feral prior to the fire.

Casey and kitten Ginger. Casey was rescued by Don Proia and
GeorgeAnn Hemingway-Proia.

Doll Stanley with a portion of our poster
board.

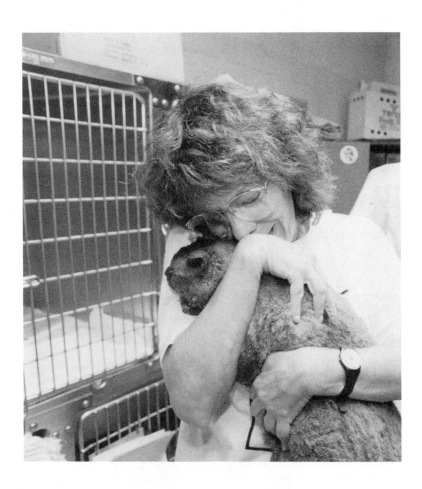

Norma Armon and Charmian as they were reunited. (Photo by Lloyd Francis, Jr., and San Jose Mercury News)

Part Three:
NEVER GIVE UP

November 1991

Throughout the ensuing weeks, the volume of animals did not decline as had been predicted by the Oakland Animal Shelter. Instead, even more pets were being found in and around the fire zone. It was only a few weeks later, although it seemed like much longer, and people became impatient and anxious about locating their lost pets. The volunteers tried to impress upon the survivors that this was a very, very small amount of time. Food and water were being put out on a regular basis all over the hills and most of it was being consumed, giving everyone proof that there were still animals up there, either domestic or wild. One day, during the first week of the month, I was in a small culvert near West View Place. I was amazed to see buds appearing on a charred branch. New life among all of this devastation. How hopeful it was to see such a thing, to know that this bush had somehow survived down at its core and was now pushing forth growth meant for another season.

Everyone looking for a pet was advised above all else not to give up. Scared and displaced pets would be returning as so many already had and the people who had lost their homes must go up and search the surrounding terrain for their pets. Many called in professional animal searchers and in their desperation, even psychics were hired by some. One woman looking for her dog, Erno, had a psychic flown in from another state. The psychic claimed that Erno was alive and roaming the hills looking for his mistress. Apparently the woman who hired the psychic did not really believe in such things, but in her desperation, she decided to try any means to find her lost friend. She never did.

Since there were no familiar items or landmarks for a wandering pet to help it find its way back home, the survivors were encouraged to leave an article of their clothing near the feeding site on their lot. This, we believed, would help spark a pet's recollection and hopefully keep it nearby if it recognized a familiar scent. How effective this strategy was is impossible to say. Many pets did manage to return to what used to be their homes, so perhaps the added scent of their owners' belongings helped them find their way back.

We began to get to know the regulars when they came into the center. Each time we would hear about another reunion we would share it with those who were still coming to look at the photographs of the found pets. For some, it was like a shot in the arm. The story of a reunion would rejuvenate their sagging spirits and fortify their search efforts. As the shock of the disaster wore off for people, more came to file reports in person. Still more called the Hotline.

The volume of calls and visits to the photo books increased daily as the word spread about the rescue. Local and national columnists called and interviewed the volunteers about the operation. Local television stations were alerted when a reunion was imminent and participated if the owner agreed. One such reunion was captured by the local ABC affiliate, KGO-TV in San Francisco.

In mid-November the television program Inside Edition came to Oakland to cover the story of the Pet Rescue. The fact that we were getting national coverage thrilled everyone because every mention of us in the media brought more people in to file reports and look at the pictures. All we wanted to do was to get the word out that we were sponsoring an organized pet rescue, and we wanted it to reach as far as possible.

The volume of pets found was increasing as were the numbers of people filing reports, yet the rate of reunions was not as high as expected. Somehow, there was beginning to be a surplus of found pets who had not been reported lost. The group desperately searching and the group of found animals did not "match." I had been certain that we would have reunited at least eighty percent of the animals found in the first two weeks, but the opposite was true. Like everyone else, I was baffled. The found animals were indisputedly from the fire; many were covered with soot, singed or burned, and had been found right in the middle of all the devastation. Yet, no one had filed a report on them. The volunteers working on the project wondered if many of these animals had belonged to people who had died in the fire, but upon investigation we found that those pets were already accounted for.

Among the regulars who came to look at the photo books was Diana Ragen. She reported on Pumpkin's progress and every day it seemed as if she had a good prognosis to give us. Diana was still looking for her other two

cats, Samantha and Sundae. Whenever we heard someone claim that their cat couldn't have survived, we told
them about Pumpkin and about Max.We'd explain to
people that cats are small and low to the ground and can
run under the smoke. We have all been taught that in case
of a fire we should drop to the ground and crawl, because
the clear air is down there. Cats and small dogs are already
down in the clear air, so their chances of surviving a fire
are already better than those of larger animals and humans. If the animal were outdoors, its chances increased,
but we told the people whose pets were indoors about Max
and encouraged them to keep looking. There is no doubt
that animals with better circumstances than Max's must
have perished in the fire, but to find a cat who had been
locked indoors and was now recovering was reassuring.

Paul Bentz was one of the people who made the
rounds of the four shelters and then came to look at the
photo books. He intensely scrutinized each photo that
might be a match with one of his cats, Nikki and Webber.
Webber was all black, but Nikki had distinctive markings
that could easily identify him. One day, not long after we
began at the One Stop Center, Paul came in with a drawing he had done of Nikki. It showed the tabby's unusual
concentric ring markings on his sides, which looked like
bull's-eye targets. He also had large tufts of lighter colored fur protruding from his ears, making him look like a
bobcat. Paul was certain that anyone would recognize
Nikki and had given copies of the drawing to all the shelters. He posted one on our bulletin board that was now
covered with pleas from people looking for their lost pets.

Phil Stanley and George Perko had reluctantly returned from London. The only reason that they had come
back was to try to locate Marduk. Phil, like many others

who had lost pets, did not feel in his heart that Marduk had persihed. Marduk's bizarre behavior in the two weeks prior to the fire led Phil to believe that the cat had been aware of something and had thus refused to come indoors for fear of being trapped. Originally, Phil had only thought of earthquakes, never imagining a firestorm. The fact that he had been awakened by two explosions that no one else had heard, made him believe that he had some sort of connection to the destruction of his house. Although he could not pinpoint the exact minute that his house had blown up on Gravatt Drive, it was very close to the period in which he had heard the explosions in London. Marduk felt alive to him and that is really the only reason he returned to California. He and George went to all of the shelters on the day that they arrived back in Oakland. Then they spotted a picture in *The Montclarion*, a local newspaper, that looked just like Marduk. They rushed to the Oakland shelter to claim thier little friend, but he was not there. No one at the shelter had any knowledge of this particular cat. The cat had been labelled in the paper as having been found three days after the fire on Golden Gate Avenue, on the other end of the fire zone from where their house was.

Phil and George were staying with some friends in a guest bedroom and Phil believed that Marduk would not be found until they had a home for him. He and George made an offer on a house. On that same day, the Hotline called about a possible match. The next morning, the bid on the house was accepted, and Marduk was reunited with his family.

As it turned out, Marduk had been the first cat trapped by Doll Stanley (no relation to Phil). He was taken to Berkeley Humane. Marduk was only about a block up Gravatt

Drive when he was found. Gravatt is in Berkeley's jurisdiction for postal addresses, but is actually in Oakland. An error somewhere along the way gave Phil and George photographic proof that Marduk was alive, but no one seemed to know what shelter he'd been taken to.

About this time, the cat that was found caring for a seriously injured cat was reunited with its owner. He was unable to give us any clues to help us identify the other cat, who had been euthanized by the Animal Shelter in Oakland because of the severity of its injuries, but we were all touched by the compassion his cat had shown for the dying stranger.

Ron and Carol Hofmann and their daughter, Stacey, returned regularly to the site of their home in the 800 block of Mountain Boulevard. The fire had stopped shortly after consuming their house, and they believed it was feasible that their five cats, Max, a year-old Flamepoint Siamese, Cindy, Nellie, Nadia, and Natasha, an older female Siamese, had made it to safe ground a few blocks away to the south. Ron and Carol had not seen any of the cats that day as they fled. Leaving with less than ten minutes notice early that afternoon, they took their thirteen-year-old dog, Mandy, with them, having forgotten in the ensuing panic the important papers and family mementos and photographs that they had hastily collected to take with them.

Three days after the fire, as rain fell all too late on the blackened hillsides, Ron and Carol found Cindy on their lot, and took her to their temporary living quarters. Doing everything possible to locate the rest of their cat family, Ron and Carol built a shelter on their property and left food, water and pieces of their clothing.

Every day, Stacey bundled up her two-year-old son and her newborn baby and made the rounds of the shelters looking for the four cats who were still missing.

The moratorium on euthanization of all animals at the Oakland Animal Shelter took effect in early November. Although they were no longer actively searching for animals, any stray pets that might be turned in to them would not be euthanized for at least a month. Now the majority of the rescue effort could be directed towards finding and reuniting the pets with the owners instead of worrying that they would be destroyed. Time was a necessary element and because of the direct efforts of many of the animal groups, especially FOCAS (Friends of Oakland City Animal Shelter), time was now on our side. The rescue could proceed as necessary without the terrifying aspect of euthanization. The effectiveness of this move in the small amount of time in which it was done is commendable.

The very first reports of lost and found pets were quickly drawn up by hand and run off on a copy machine. Although intentions were good, certain items were overlooked and it made followup difficult. Many of the spaces to be filled in on the forms were much too small and people tried to squeeze in as much information as they could. This made the reports difficult to read and the information required not extensive enough. Sometimes a cat was listed as "gray male with a collar." Whether or not he was neutered, declawed, or had other colors, former scars or injuries was not noted. Sometimes a very identifiable trait, such as the color of the collar, was not on the form. As the weeks rolled on, the forms were revised and entered into a computer, but the fields for information were still too limited and further complicated the procedure when printed out. The computer was quickly abandoned.

Four weeks after the fire, the appearance of a number of found cats had changed significantly and a photographer took additional pictures of them. One of the original finds, nicknamed "Crispy" because of his appearance, posed once again. His picture had been in the newspapers and on television, yet no one had claimed him. One of the new pictures showed his coat, which was now growing back.

Paul Bentz looked at the picture and said that the cat was the same color as Nikki, so we made a notation on his report to refer to that picture in order to clarify the color of his cat. Because the cat did not have the distinctive bull's-eye markings, Paul did not further consider it. I urged him to go to the shelter and look at the cat anyway, just in case.

"I've seen this cat every time that I've been there," he told me, "and it's not my cat. It always sits at the back of the cage, ignoring everyone."

Again I encouraged Paul to look closer at this cat the next time he went to the shelter. He stared at the photo once more before he left.

The next evening, we had people lined up three deep at the tables straining to see the photos, when I saw Paul at the back of the crowd. He pointed over everyone towards the books and said in a quiet and strained voice, cracking with emotion, "It's my cat."

"What?" I said in surprise.

"That cat, the one that I said had the same color as my cat. It's Nikki."

Everyone stopped and gathered around as Paul told what had happened. He had seen the cat every time that he had been at the shelter, probably every other day for the past four weeks, about a dozen or more times. It showed none of Nikki's physical traits, and although its fur was singed, there was no bull's-eye pattern. On this last visit to the shelter he walked up to the cage and called out the cat's name. He responded immediately and almost came through the bars at him!

"Paul, this cat has been in all the papers, and is considered to be our 'poster cat.' You must have seen him on television."

"I don't have a television anymore. I lost it in the fire," Paul said. He had made a good point. It showed me that there were people out there that were not getting our message because they did not have the means to do so. Many of them had lived through something so horrible that they did not want any further references to it and might be avoiding such things as reports related to the fire. After all, they had seen it firsthand and did not need to be told about it.

Paul immediately sat down and intensely scrutinized the photos again, wondering if he had overlooked Webber, as well. Webber was a big male, solid black. Paul especially studied any cats labelled "gray," assuming Webber's coat might be covered with enough ash to turn him gray.

Among the saddest of the searchers were those who had lost family members in the fire. A number of them came to the One Stop Center to take care of the necessary business and would stop by to see the pictures. One young woman had lost her mother-in-law and her sister-in-law. The family had found the dog's collar in the ashes, which confirmed its demise, yet she still came in to search for the two cats. Her concern gave the volunteers a better sense of what lengths people would go to to have the animals returned to their care.

We did have a problem, although not a major one, with "look alikes." I assisted in the trapping of a very angry black and white cat on Gravatt Drive. The unusual markings on the cat's face reminded me of a clown's makeup. It looked as if a big clown's nose were drawn over the cat's own nose. Later that day, before the picture was even placed in the book, a middle-aged couple came to look for their black and white cat. They told me that he did not have a very friendly personality. I described the cat that was now at Berkeley Humane and apologized for the "clown" reference. The couple was ecstatic; that is exactly how they would describe their cat, they said. I also mentioned a small black dot on the cat's face. I went to retrieve the picture from the file. Upon seeing the photograph, they were certain that it was their cat, especially when I related how angry he was at being in the trap. Off they went with a promise to call the next day when they went to the shelter to collect the unhappy boy.

When they did not call, I phoned them, as I was anxious to know how the cat had responded to them. I was shocked when the husband told me that it was not their cat. He said that the markings were almost identical and that he could not believe that any other cat in the world had such a bizarre look, but upon seeing the cat in person, they were positive that it was not theirs.

The volunteers now emphasized in every encounter that although a pet may look just like yours, you absolutely had to go see it before declaring a reunion. We carefully made sure that each person was aware of the possibilities that even the pets who looked like theirs in the photographs might turn out not to be. It was tough to temper the excitement of someone who had just flipped a page and seen a familiar face staring back at him. Instead of our usual elation, our advice was now to "go and see" and then we could celebrate if, in fact, the animal in question turned out to be the one they were seeking. Given the situation, we wanted everyone to be hopeful, but not to place every expectation upon an animal that might not be theirs. We did not want to be responsible for broken hearts. Many reunions did occur, but there were a number of mistaken identities, such as happened to the couple with the black and white cat.

Jimmy Reina and Elaine Gerber had lost everything except for their pets, when their house on Capricorn Avenue had burned. Now that they had their animals back, they could face putting their lives back together. Jimmy still could not believe how luck had placed him behind the fire lines that night, how he had found one cat, Simi, sleeping in the dog's bed, and how he had grabbed Mamalucci as he was diving over the fence. The couple found a new home near their old one. A friend had a home for rent, and they took it. It overlooked one of the regional parks along the crest of the hills behind the fire zone. Within two weeks of moving into their new home, however, Mamalucci had disappeared.

Jimmy was especially distraught. He had saved Mamalucci that awful night as the fire bore down upon their home, and now he was gone. It was a twist of fate that was difficult for Jimmy to bear. He relentlessly searched all of the shelters, veterinarians, animal hospitals, and animal rescue foundations. He filed reports with the Pet Rescue Hotline and came to look at the photo books on a regular basis. He canvassed his neighborhood and put up posters asking for any information to find the cat.

At Berkeley Humane Society, a dirty, blackened cat that had just been trapped in Hiller Highlands was brought in and placed in a viewing cage. A half hour later, Ethel King, while on one of her regular trips to the shelter, took one look at the bedraggled cat and knew that under all that grime was her beloved friend, Gallagher. With tears of relief, she opened the cage and scooped the soot-stained cat into her arms.

It was about this time in November that some of the residents of Marlborough Terrace first noticed the large German Shepherd mix standing among the ruins. As they sifted through the debris trying to find any remnants of their possessions, the dog would watch them from a safe distance on the higher side of the street.

No amount of coaxing would bring the dog any closer than a few lots. Solitarily, it sat, as if waiting for the return of its absent owner. Bob and Ingrid Cole, among the first to see the dog, had no recollection of it ever having been in the neighborhood before. They knew practically everyone on the street, and everyone's pet. The dog would not respond to anyone and kept its silent vigil on different lots along the street, refusing any and all offers of human contact.

No one was certain how long the rescue effort would continue. Doll had been committed to searching and trapping in the hills for one month, and as that month closed, the period was extended. The amount of animals being found was increasing as the weeks passed. Initially, we thought that the bulk of lost pets would be located immediately after the fire, but the reverse was true. Up to ten cats a day were being found in the traps as more came out of their hiding places and covered more territory in a search for food. Dogs were still being sighted as they ran across the barren landscape.

Although the area had been levelled by the fire, there were still nooks and crannies where small animals could hide very easily. Slabs of concrete and foundations still existed as did large chunks of unrecognizable debris. The terrain of the hills had lots of little valleys and hidden spots across the nineteen hundred acres.

Since this rescue was the first of its kind, there were not any previous procedures on which to rely for guidance. Each issue had to be addressed and dealt with as it arose. Some of us thought that all the animals would have been found and reunited within a month. Daily, we could see that this was an overly ambitious hope on our part. Not all were being found yet and there were many still unclaimed. Pets were being trapped every day who had not been reported lost to us. The Hotline was in operation over forty hours per week and deluged with calls, yet here was a surplus of animals, and not just a few. It seemed as if the majority of the found ones were not being claimed. Thankfully, housing these animals did not prove to be too difficult. Throughout the network of people in all the various animal groups, shelter was quickly arranged in foster homes for the ever increasing numbers of pets being found.

Almost on a day-by-day basis, it was decided to extend the rescue. The enormity of the job became more apparent after the first thirty days. Suddenly, Thanksgiving was upon us, but we stood firm and just continued as we had been. Then three major stumbling blocks occurred almost simultaneously.

The city of Oakland needed the space which we had been using at the One Stop Center and we would have to find another location to display the photo books. The space which the Pet Rescue Hotline was occupying was needed by Berkeley Humane Society and another location would have to be found for that phase of the operation, too. Then, the month-long euthanization moratorium expired and about one hundred pets were in danger of being killed very shortly. This was the most critical of our problems. The group EBAR (East Bay Animal Referral) stepped in and took charge of bailing out the threatened pets. The shelter had decided to put them up for adoption on the basis of the first to come into the shelter would be the first available. The fine folks at EBAR did not differentiate and took out all the animals every day. EBAR did not have the funds to support such an endeavor, nor did any of the other groups, so the EBAR volunteers used their own money to save these pets and find them foster care. Many of these people ran their credit cards up to the maximum limit try-ing to save these lives. Their diligent efforts truly rank them among the unsung heroes of this catastrophe.

Nancy Rogers kept going back up to her property to try to find her cat Princess. She had no doubt that the calico cat had survived in spite of the enormous devasta-tion all around her. After their miraculous reunion with her son's dog, Bud, at their church, Nancy felt confident Princess was out there waiting to be found. In the latter part of November, while on her way back down the hill from her property, something made Nancy stop and look at the big tree under which she had sought shelter during the first part of the firestorm. There was a poster with Polaroid photos of recently found pets from that neighborhood, which Doll Stanley had placed there. Nancy parked and walked over to inspect the photos. The second one she saw was unmistakably Princess. She had known in her heart that it was only a matter of time before she found her, and now it was true. She called the Hotline to claim Princess. The feisty cat had been an ungracious houseguest at two foster homes and greeted Nancy with her characteristic nonchalance.

Jay Stewart, another person who had sought refuge under the spreading tree at the same intersection had finally found a suitable apartment, although it did not accept pets. Chad, his twelve-year-old retriever, was still missing, so he signed the lease. He returned to his temporary housing to find a message: Chad had been found. Jay, ecstatic, was in a dilemma. He had just signed a lease in good faith, telling the management he did not have a pet. In addition to that, there was a woman who had been scheduled to adopt Chad that afternoon. As Chad gleefully greeted Jay, he made an agreement with the woman. She would foster Chad, and Jay could have the dog on weekends until his house was rebuilt. Jay explained the situation to the new landlords of his multi-unit building and they suggested that Jay simply use another entrance during that time. Under the circumstances, they would look the other way. It was a win-win-win situation. Jay had the apartment and Chad. The woman who wanted Chad so much would have him, too. Chad would have someone with him during the day to care for him while Jay went to work. Everything had worked out to the satisfaction of all concerned.

The more animals being found and rescued from the shelters, the more the numbers of unclaimed animals increased. All were placed in foster care or adoptive homes with the provision that if the owner should be located within a reasonable amount of time, the adoptive person would relinquish the pet to them.

The foster care was arranged through several animal groups, and many of the actual members of these groups provided shelter for the pets. At this point, there was no shortage of homes willing to care for these displaced pets and every pet was placed. This was not done in a haphazard fashion. Everyone had to be screened. In some cases, a volunteer would personally vouch for another person, thus eliminating some of the screening process. No "open adoptions" were held where the pet was just given to the next available person who was willing to adopt it. The process was conducted with a maximum of concern for the animal's welfare above all else.

It was assumed that these pets would eventually be reunited with the people who had lost them, so the foster/adoptive person was forewarned of this eventuality. There were specific rules which had to be adhered to and a signed agreement was mandatory. Dogs must be confined on a run or in a securely fenced yard, and cats must remain indoors at all times.

Under the circumstances, if a situation did not seem to be working out, the Pet Rescue would take the pet back and find other lodgings for it. This was a guarantee that made many foster people feel much better. We would even try to provide a pick up for the animal. We were so very grateful that these people had agreed to take these animals into their homes and to care for them that we wanted to make it as easy as possible for them. Sometimes things did not work out, but there were few cases where we had to find other homes after the initial one. After all, these were traumatized animals who had gone through a major disaster with varying degrees of distress. Most people, when we checked in to be updated on the placement, told us that they would be willing to permanently adopt the pet. Many hinted that even if the original owner was located, it would be difficult to give the pet back.

On the other hand, many of the owners claimed that if the pet were found, and had a good, loving home, they could bear to leave it there. All they wanted to know was that the animal had survived and was all right and was happy in the new environment. From all sides, it was the pet's well-being that mattered the most.

The moves for the Hotline and the photo book project took place in early December.

The Pet Rescue Hotline moved into a space donated by Heymann Properties. Henrietta Obendoerfer, who runs Heymann, had lost her home in the fire and was searching for her two cats. The space, formerly a bedroom of a turn-of-the-century home, was more than ample for the desks, files and telephones. The Hotline was still operating on a daily basis and calls still flooded the lines. The photo books were now on view at the Montclair Women's Club at the corner of Thornhill and Mountain Boulevard. The club was adjacent to Highways 13 and 24, and actually only three blocks from where the fire had ended.

Graciously assisting the community when it was needed, the club generously gave us a large room with an open-ended invitation to stay as long as we wished. Some of the members of the club had lost their homes in the fire and unanimously voted to donate the space. Jaye Ashford, the club manager, took care of the paperwork and other necessities associated with acquiring such a space, allowing us to go on with the project. The Montclair Women's

Club is a well-known local landmark, so directions and explanations about location were minimal for those who would come to see the new photographs.

Those who came by were concerned that so much time had elapsed since the fire. It did seem that way, although it was less than eight weeks since it had happened. Concerns were raised about the welfare of pets still in the hills now that the colder weather had arrived.

All we could hope was that it might force more of them to come out of hiding. Intermittent rain had fallen, but nothing of significance. California faced yet another year of drought.The meteorologists did not foresee a relief from so many years of sub-normal rainfall. There would be wet days but not enough of them. Most of the people who had been residents of the fire zone hoped that the drought would continue. Excessive rainfall meant landslides. Hydroseeding had already taken place in the zone, covering everything with a layer of hay that looked like it had been dipped in mint Mylanta.

Anyone who was searching for a beloved pet dreaded the thought of a cold, wet winter. They were assured that food and water were being left out for them, but shelter was another issue. Pampered cats and dogs who had never been left outdoors now faced fending on their own for the first time in their lives. The trappers were doing all that they could, but traumatized animals were moving about the zone, not staying in one place, as they restlessly searched for food and their families. Obviously, those who had survived were so distrustful of these strangers wandering about with traps, that they became more elusive.

The trappers repeatedly found raccoons and possums in the traps. They were released, of course, unless they were injured. In that case, they were taken to a wildlife trauma center for treatment. The presence of wild animals was a very good sign. In just short of sixty days after this horrible conflagration, the wildlife had returned to this area. Deer were seen, gingerly climbing the hillsides. If wildlife could survive, then perhaps the domestic pets could as well. A lot of the wildlife must have fled and could have remained very easily in the vast regional parks just adjacent to the zone, but there they were, trying to resume life in their former neighborhoods, too. All along, food had been left out for them, but now arrangements were made to have more nutritious and appropriate food delivered to strategic spots for their survival.

It was not a happy holiday season. Many people seemed to just go through the motions. It was a draining effort for most people to even think about holidays under the best of circumstances. Now faced with the loss of everything they owned and having to rebuild their lives, many people did not celebrate.

In mid-December, Jan Hennault, one of the volunteers, arranged to have a television program produced about the rescue. It was done in a panel discussion format. Doll took off time from her trapping schedule to join Connie Cwynar, Yvette Resnick, Ellie Hoffmann, and me as we explained exactly what we were trying to accomplish.

We explained how we were running the rescue and the situation as it now stood, that we were finding a number of animals who had not been claimed. The main message of the show was that we were still in operation and that we needed people to come forward and file reports. We related various stories, showing the pictures in the photo books, and explained that many more animals had survived than previously estimated. We stressed that although the particular pet's situation might have seemed hopeless, it was not necessarily the case. There were numerous stories of incredible survival told with the hope that someone might see the program or hear about it from someone else and come forward to a happy reunion. What had seemed like a lot of time to fill almost evaporated and the thirty-minute program was over in no time. For the next couple of months, the program aired intermittently on local cable access with very positive feedback to the producer.

Many reunions were not dramatic. Sometimes, a cat or dog was trapped, taken to Pet Rescue at Berkeley Humane and a report was written up. When it was compared to the reports of lost pets on file, the possible matches were listed and the people called and asked to come and see the pet. Many reunions happened just that way. More pets were returning to their home sites as well and the Hotline often received a call that the lost pet had just shown up. Almost daily, someone was able to write "Reunited" diagonally in red across a report and place it into another file. It was the greatest reward for our efforts to know that one of the surviving pets was now back with its people. What we had set out to do was being accomplished with some degree of success.

The year of 1991 turned into 1992 without much sentimentality among anyone who was associated with the disaster. It had been the worst residential fires in the history of the United States, and while the tallies of the monetary losses were still being estimated, the loss of human and animal lives could never be rationalized.

With the new year came the fresh hope that more of the lost pets would be located. It had been three months since the fire. For some, the time that had passed put a different perspective on what they had gone through, a landmark of sorts. For others, it was just more time that they had been separated from their companions. The fear that the pet would not be found grew with each week. The winter rains had begun in earnest and the desolate, burned hillsides were pelted with the storms. Although the official word by January was that rainfall was still significantly below normal, it was difficult to tell that to someone whose cat had lived its life wholly indoors and now might be having to deal with the elements for the first time.

It was not knowing that really gnawed at people. They only wanted an answer about their pets. Maybe someone had found it and did not know about the Hotline; maybe it had died and was cremated where it had perished; maybe it was still out there, alone, hungry, cold. The new home could be visited, the death could be grieved, but an animal alone in winter, even a "mild" California one, was unbearable for the pet owners. Northern California winters are not the idyllic ones that Southern California experiences. Because of their placement across the Bay from San Francisco, Oakland and Berkeley are subject to many of the same weather conditions, especially the fogs. A finger of fog can be seen being pulled across the Bay by the meteoric forces of pressure and air streams and pulled up over the East Bay hills, giving the area the same cold, gray dripping fog that is so picturesque in descriptions of San Francisco. Spreading over the charred landscape of the Oakland/Berkeley hills, the fog's effect is not only eerie, but cold and inhospitable. The winds, which did so much to promote the fire in October, now swept across the barren open spaces. Occasionally, snow falls in the higher elevations, visible from the San Francisco Bay Area.

The local media were still interested in the stories about the reunions. One night toward the end of January,

KTVU, the Oakland station, broadcast a piece about some of the recently found pets. The next day, a family who has requested anonymity, came forward to claim their cat who had been trapped only days before, and whom they had seen on the television show. They had never bothered to file a report with the Hotline because they mistakenly assumed that the cat had perished in the fire.

Shortly after that, one of the volunteers was combing through the reports of found animals and something looked amiss. A cat who had been reported to us very early in the rescue effort as a "part Siamese" was wearing a tag with a Los Angeles resident's name—Bob P.— and a telephone number. The number had been out of service for some time and the name of the owner did not have a listing in either the Los Angeles area or in the area surrounding Oakland. It had been found in the rear yard of a home on Swainland Road just off of Broadway Terrace, inside the edge of the fire perimeter.

With her sharp eye for detail, Rose Lernberg had noticed and remembered that a cat had been lost who was wearing a tag with a Los Angeles phone number. Looking back at the reports, Rose found one for a tricolor cat that had on a white flea collar and a heart shaped tag with her name "Samantha" and a notation of an "L.A. #." The cat was Diana Ragen's.

Rose called Diana and pieced together the clues that led to the reunion.

Samantha had originally belonged to Bob P. Diana had adopted the cat about a year and a half before the fire, but had not changed the tag. She had seen the report on this cat every time that she had come in to look at the pictures and reports, but had never looked further than the main description of the cat being "part Siamese." It was an understandable oversight. Samantha was not part Siamese nor did she look it to anyone other than the person who found her, who had attempted to describe her as best as possible. It was an error that was a matter of interpretation, but it ended happily for Diana Ragen. Samantha was her second cat out of three to be found. Pumpkin was undergoing plastic surgery to correct the injuries she had suffered on her journey as she transversed the fire zone. It appeared that Samantha had gone in another direction and had escaped to the outer edges of the conflagration. The family who had found her had taken good care of her and she had gained a significant amount of weight during her absence.

In spite of the seemingly futile act of filing a report, John and Christine O'Connell still did so on the three feral cats that lived on their deck. The young couple did not feel comfortable forgetting about the mother cat and her two offspring who had shared the Upper Broadway Terrace home with them for the past three years.

They had evacuated with their own "indoor" cat, Roscoe, as the fire swept towards their home, but had not seen any of the feral cats. Even if they had, it would have been impossible to rescue them. Even with ample time and under optimum circumstances, catching the three would have been very difficult. On the day of the fire, it was not even a consideration. There had been precious little time after Chris arrived home before they'd had to leave.

All three cats were terrified of people. The O'Connells first saw the feral kittens when the mother moved them from the blackberry bushes to a neighbor's basement during a rainstorm shortly after they had moved into the house.

Not wanting to let a nursing mother starve, they bought cat food and began to feed them. They named the mother Momcat and the kittens Smokey and Blackie. Throughout the ensuing months, the O'Connells took pictures of the cats, which were in the photo albums that they took with them as they fled the firestorm. Thus, they were able to furnish the Hotline with pictures. Three months after the fire when Doll Stanley trapped a cat very close to where their house had been, the volunteers were able to determine that it was probably Blackie. When Christine O'Connell was told that Blackie might have been located, she was thrilled but warned everyone that the cat was wild and to handle her with care.

Much to everyone's surprise, Blackie was not reacting in a feral manner when the O'Connells went to identify her. She was docile and friendly. Thinking that this might be a very close look-alike, a comparison with the photo taken before the fire proved beyond a doubt that this was indeed the same cat. In addition, the cat was found within a hundred feet of where the house had stood.

Blackie's behavior continued to amaze the family. She readily formed a bond with the O'Connell's two-year-old son, Scott. Although she never liked to be picked up, Scott is allowed to do so without any protestations from her. She no longer wants to be outdoors and prefers to stay inside. Blackie amazed everyone when she curled up in John's lap for the first time. Now, she has become a loving "lap" cat who patiently tolerates Scott's playtimes with her. The turnaround in Blackie's personality has made her a very welcome member of the family.

February can be an especially sweet month in northern California. There have been summer months that were somehow misplaced and arrived in February. It is as if nature needs a break from winter and bestows a vacation upon the area with warm sunshine and clear azure skies. Alternatively, there have been Februarys that were only an extension of dreary January. February 1992 began as an extension for a couple of weeks and then the weather turned exquisite. During the last week in the month, the temperatures were in the high seventies.

On Marlborough Terrace, the Shepherd-mix dog carefully eyed the workmen who were beginning to remove dried out foundations in preparation to rebuild some of the homes. Some of the construction workers tossed scraps of their sandwiches to the dog, who moved cautiously up to the morsel, and more cautiously sniffed it before devouring it. The dog was always there and it was assumed that it was from the neighborhood and had returned to its former home. Rain or sunshine, the dog was seen, never moving from a radius of more than two or three home sites.

The Hotline still received numerous reports of missing animals every day. Kathryn Howell, who was one of the early volunteers, was amazed at the volume of calls. The reports of found pets grew as well, as people called in to say that they thought that they were harboring a potential animal fire victim. We were grateful that these pets were in foster homes, since the space at Berkeley Humane Society was very limited.

Every day, Doll and John and the other trappers found at least three cats and an occasional dog in the hills. Instead of decreasing, the numbers were still increasing. The magnitude of the rescue was overwhelming.

It was supposed that all the dogs that had been within the zone had been located. None had been seen for quite a while. It was almost exclusively cats which now had to be found. By this time, we realized that many of the found animals would not be reunited with their people. There were over one hundred and fifty, mainly cats, who survived the inferno only to be left unclaimed. We suspected that the owners just did not believe that their animals could have lived through such a monumental disaster and had not even bothered to look for them. We hoped that perhaps we had found these beautiful animals better, more deserving homes, where they would be loved and not forgotten.

One rainy Saturday, Sue McEneany and I had to deliver something to another site in Oakland. Since she has lived there and was more familiar with the area, she offered to drive. The quickest way to our destination was across the fire zone. The gray wetness of the sky blended into the somber ashen surroundings. We finished our chore and on our way back to the Montclair Women's Club we stopped to check on one of the feeding sites on Grandview Drive. As soon as I turned to get back into the car, I spotted two dogs, one a large Australian Shepherd sort and the other an indeterminate mix who was small, shaggy and a light gray color. I thought that the smaller dog might have been white at one time. Sue and I tried to gently coax the two dogs to us, but they would have no part of it. For every step we took, they retreated a step. The smaller dog kept watching the larger one for direction. I knew that we might have only this one chance to see them, so I memorized each feature that might give us a clue. Seconds later, they disappeared around a curve, and that was the last that we saw of them. We walked all over the area, thinking that they might be a workman's dogs, but there were no other vehicles nearby. When we got back to the club, we checked the reports, and sure enough there were three other sightings of the Shepherd, and some possible sightings of the smaller dog.

The next day, one that was wetter than the previous one, Sue went up to the street where we had last seen the dogs and looked for them. She crawled under a concrete slab that supported part of a swimming pool thinking that they might be hiding out there. Equipped with a tarpaulin to shield her from the rain, Sue sat at that spot for over four hours hoping to catch the dogs. She has a special way with animals and has had deer eat from her hands, so she felt that maybe the dogs would come to her. Unfortunately, they were never seen again. That day, I called four people who had filed reports on missing dogs that fit the descriptions, and I was surprised to meet with various reactions which ranged from "I'll get up there tomorrow if it's not raining" to "We have a new puppy." One person told me to call back when we had trapped the dogs. I tried to explain that the dogs would come to them before they would come to a stranger, and that it was important that the owner get up there and search as well, not to leave it exclusively to the volunteers. The rescue effort could only go so far. I don't know if the dogs were ever reunited with their owners.

Most of the people who were looking for their animals were adamant that we call them at any time of the day or night if there was even the most remote possibility of a match, and they would go right away to see if it was their pet. Two of these people were Elaine Gerber and Jimmy Reina who were still looking for Mamalucci. By the end of February, Jimmy really began to wonder if they would ever see Mamalucci again. He still made the rounds of the shelters a couple of times per week. After rescuing Mamalucci the night of the fire, Jimmy was not about to give up after the cat's subsequent disappearance.

In the first few days of March, the Hotline received a call from a woman named Celeste who had been hiking in Tilden Park two days earlier. She had seen a cat wearing a green collar, so she knew that it could not be one of the feral cats that inhabited the park. The description fit that of Mamalucci, so the Hotline called Jimmy and Elaine and gave them Celeste's telephone number.

The three met early the next evening at the entrance to the park. There had been a thunderstorm during the night, so Jimmy and Elaine seriously doubted if Mamalucci would be around. Celeste led them to the point where she had spotted the cat three days earlier. It was over six and a half miles from where they had last seen Mamalucci. As they looked over the extensive vista, Jimmy and Elaine knew that it would be like looking for the proverbial needle in the haystack. Jimmy wandered ahead of the two women, searching under the bushes. Suddenly, Celeste ran up to him and excitedly told him that the cat was in exactly the same place where she had seen him before. It was Mamalucci. He cautiously stretched towards Elaine who had some food to coax him, and when he was within her reach, she grabbed him. Instead of being happy at being reunited with his family, Mamalucci went berserk. He bit Elaine's hands through the soft flesh between her thumb and forefinger, and in his terror, wet all over her. Elaine knew that if she let go, they would never see Mamalucci again. They had saved him from the inferno, lost him, and now had him back again. In spite of the intense pain of the bite, Elaine did not let go.

They wrestled the struggling cat into the carrier that they had brought with them, and miraculously, Mamalucci calmed down immediately, becoming his former self. After seeking medical treatment for Elaine, they then took

Mamalucci to the veterinarian's. His weight had dropped to four pounds from his normal nine and one half.

That night, exhausted, injured, but extremely happy to have been reunited with Mamalucci, Elaine and Jimmy picked up a take out-order of Chinese food. At the end of the meal, Jimmy gleefully read his fortune cookie message to Elaine. It said: "He that seeks shall find." The tiny slip of paper and the map showing the remarkable distance which Mamalucci traveled during his hiatus are proudly displayed on the wall of Jimmy and Elaine's new home. It serves as a testament to their staunch determination to find the cat that they refused to lose.

Although over four months had passed since the Firestorm, the numbers of animals being found did not really slacken by this time. Cats were still being found regularly in the baited traps across the hills. Reunions such as Mamalucci's with his owners, encouraged all of those who were working on the rescue, proving that it was vital not to give up hope under any circumstances. Winston Churchill may have summed it up best during a World War II speech when he stated, "Never, never, never, never, never give up." Hopes could diminish and the possibility that the pet did not survive was a very real one, but having seen so many unusual situations occurring during these past months, it was a great incentive to keep the rescue effort in operation. Who knew what pet might turn up next?

Many residents of the fire zone had begun rebuilding. Almost all of the foundations had dried out in the intense heat and were useless and had to be removed as a first step in clearing the lot. The debris from the fire—the twisted bits of metal and roof tiles and glass mingled with

the ash —had been cleared away by April under direct or-
ders from both city governments. Each resident had been
charged if they had not already contracted to have the remnants hauled away. The foundations could remain in place
until it was time to rebuild. This work disturbed a number
of animals who had hidden out like outlaws, and it also
drove a lot of them to deal with the human rescuers.

The movement of the animals was understandable,
but the movement of the people made our job especially
difficult. When filling out their reports, some had put only
the name of the hotel where they were staying just after
the disaster. Others gave numbers of friends who did not
know where the survivors were presently staying. The post
office would forward for a year, but some reports only listed
the street where the loss had occurred, not the house number. Many people had unlisted telephone numbers. In
November and again in February, we called everyone who
had filed a report to ask if the pet had been found and if
not, if they wished to continue the search. We discovered
that quite a number of the pets had returned under their
own volition and we had not been told.

April 1992

"Even if you find just one, isn't it worth it?" (A note written by a fire survivor upon learning that the rescue effort might
close.)

It came as a shock on April 6th when I was curtly
informed by Judith Cwynar that the rescue operation
would cease in two weeks, on the six-month anniversary
of the fire. Up until that time, Judith had kept control of
the entries into the photo books but did not staff the table

or deal with the survivors who came in regularly to look for their pets.

The information was given to me just as the first person was entering the Montclair Women's Club to see if there were any new pictures. I vehemently objected to bringing the effort to an end. More than that, I objected to the brief statement given by someone who was not one of the people in command. Judith told me that there would be no discussion. She claimed that she had decided to discontinue the entire operation. I offered to take complete charge of the photo books, but she absolutely refused to let me have them. The effort would cease and that was that. Yvette Resnick strenuously objected to Judith's decree as well. We told everyone who came in that night what might take place in two weeks. The look of misery on their faces was almost too much to bear. So many of them had been hanging on to this tiny thread of hope and now it was being yanked away from them. Over the months they had something to do, something to look for. Any day, one of their beloved pets might reappear and be pictured in the blue plastic albums. To give it up now, especially on the six-month anniversary compounded the pain.

I reassured each of them that I would do everything possible to keep the search going. I was certain that we could negotiate somehow. I had developed a strong rapport with a number of these people who came through the doors of the club and I felt that it was cathartic for them to have this "therapy" session to go to on a regular basis. Here, they told us the stories about their losses. The volunteers were able to reassure them that they had done all they possibly could have. Sometimes, we would hear the story again and again, but no one cared. The survivors were unburdening themselves. None of them was to blame.

Most had escaped with only the clothes on their backs, many having stayed behind until the last possible second looking for their pet.

Neither Yvette nor I glossed over the facts. Many animals had died, but we emphasized that many more than expected had survived. Cats especially found unique hiding spaces. The surplus of unclaimed animals was growing daily.

On the other hand, there was a determined group who refused to give up the search. For these folks, it was as if a family member were missing. They exhausted every possibility of finding the missing pet. Now, it appeared as though their chance would be taken away from them.

The main group sponsoring the rescue effort, In Defense of Animals, had been slowly retreating. The original time estimate had been one month, and when the scope and magnitude of the disaster grew, their commitment was extended on a month-to-month basis. They had not intended to be with this effort so long, and really had given much more than they had originally planned. The leader of the organization had determined that there were other, more important high-profile projects that necessitated the group's attention. He had only attended one function in February 1992, when an informal potluck was held for the volunteers. I doubt if he ever set foot in the fire zone, so his knowledge of what we were doing was limited to what was told to him.

Connie, her sister Judith, Diane McDermott ,and Doll Stanley were the last few hold outs from IDA. Doll had been an employee of the organization for a long time, and Connie, who had been a volunteer, was hired early in 1992. Both women had devoted many hours of their own time to the rescue effort, and understandably it was time for them to move on. IDA had been very generous in extending the time allotted for this project, but now it was not allowing the volunteers to take over and continue this important work. All I asked Judith that night was that I be allowed to continue with the rescue, but my request was denied. I became determined not to let all of the people and their pets down. Animals do not know that they are supposed to be found by a certain date. Six months—one hundred eighty days—is literally no time at all when you're dealing with a disaster of this scope. People shared their cat and dog stories with us, thus giving us a better perspective of what a small amount of time had really passed since the fire. Kathleen Kelley told me that as a child, the family's cat had routinely disappeared from their summer home on Memorial Day, reappearing when the car was being loaded and the house was being closed up near Labor Day. He had not been seen the entire time, having taken his very own vacation.

But in the case of the firestorm pets, there was nothing familiar to return to. By April the last of the lots had been cleared of debris, so any familiar items that might have attracted a pet would have been removed. Heavy equipment also frightened the animals, forcing those that might be close by to once again flee to safer territory.

The spring weather was here and the daylight hours would be extended with daylight savings time, which would make it easier for the rescues to continue. Trappers would be able to go out more and the additional daylight would allow for more time in the hills.

That night I stayed awake trying to formulate a plan whereby the effort could continue. I was not going to just close it down and walk away when I knew that there were more animals that could be reunited with their owners if we continued operating. People were depending on us to help them find those pets. Fortunately, I was not the only one who wanted to continue. On the next Thursday, a group of us met at a small restaurant in Berkeley to try to figure out how to keep this important program going. Doll Stanley, Patt Shaw, Rose Lernberg and I met to formulate a plan.

Doll was obligated to do as her employer, IDA, wanted. She immediately became a volunteer for the Pet Rescue. Berkeley Humane, the non-kill shelter, no longer had room for any more animals now that they were in their "high" season when so many unwanted puppies and kittens would be arriving, so it would be necessary to find other accommodations for animals. The Hotline would now be almost wholly independent, although still officially under the Alameda County Veterinary Association. Patt needed one more volunteer to help with the work that she and Kathryn Howell and Rose had been doing every Monday and Thursday. Without hesitation, I offered my services. I had been with the rescue effort from the beginning, and although I had not actually worked at the Hotline, I was aware of most things that had occurred. I knew the people, the animals, and the procedures.

We figured that the majority of the survivors had seen the bulk of the photos. Many came now just to see the most recent ones. Occasionally, there was a new person who had just heard about the rescue effort who came by to look, but they were rare.

Jaye Ashford, who was the on-site manager of the Montclair Women's Club had arranged for the photo book project to remain at the club indefinitely if we wished. They had been exceedingly generous throughout the months immediately following the disaster and their offer of continued support, although it was not taken, was deeply appreciated.

Instead, the photo books were turned over to the Oakland Library's History Room. Anyone who turned up to look at them would be directed there. Any new photographs of recently found animals were to be displayed in the window of California Savings & Loan on Mountain Boulevard in the Montclair section of Oakland, just up the street from the Montclair Women's Club.

I felt an enormous sense of relief that this project—so dear to my heart—would continue. I would no longer have contact with the wonderful people who came by to look at the photographs and tell their stories and concerns and that saddened me, but the rescue would continue, and I'd remain a part of it.

Just two weeks later, our determination to keep the rescue going paid off.

A female tabby who had been at Berkeley Humane for a long time still remained unidentified. Berkeley Humane thought that the cat might be feral because of various traits she exhibited towards humans.

The Hofmann family had only found one of their five cats since October, and that week Ron saw a picture of the tabby and decided to go take a look. Carol Hofmann looked at the picture and was certain it was not their cat Nellie. Something about the cat just didn't look right to her. The family's hopes of finding the remainder of their cat family were waning.

Nevertheless, Ron Hofmann decided to try anyway. He and his daughter went to the Humane society and studied the tabby. Her whiskers were burned away and her coat had a strange, waxen texture to it, as if it were coated with some thick substance. But although Ron was not sure

about the tabby's identity, she was sure of his. Upon seeing him and his daughter, the cat became suddenly gre-
garious and affectionate. She butted her head against their
outstretched hands as Nellie had always done.

Carol Hofmann was amazed and overjoyed when
Nellie was reunited with the family at their rental apartment. She and Ron wondered if their other cats still missing—Nadia, Natasha, and Max—might also have changed
so much in appearance that the Hofmann's simply hadn't
recognized their photos. Max particularly might not be
recognizable; he was only nine months old at the time of
the fire.

Such a reunion as that of Nellie and her family only
strengthened our determination to remain in operation as
long as possible. All of us realized that the numbers of
animals found would diminish as the time lengthened, but
it was necessary for us to remain in place and try to get as
many of these pets home as we possibly could. If others
had had their way, Nellie would not be home with her
people.

At the Hotline, we were very careful not to let people
get too excited when we called. Some of them assumed
that we would only call if we had definitely found their pet
and would shout for joy when we identified ourselves. We
had to rapidly tell them that we had a "long shot" even
when we were almost positive that it was a match. We had
seen too many that were so close. Besides, none of the
volunteers had ever met any of the animals, so we could
never be completely certain that there was a match.

Most people were very grateful for any possible leads
and went to investigate. Some never went, for whatever
reasons, and we could only lead them so far. A few actually got angry, but that was rare. One man told me that

these calls to check a picture or to call someone who was fostering an animal was putting him through too much anguish and pain. When I told him that I could label his file as closed and if his pet were found we would just find it another home without his knowledge, he suddenly changed his tone and requested that his file be kept open. Except for these isolated incidents everyone to whom we spoke was extremely appreciative of our work.

It was just the four of us who were actually at the Hotline now: Patt Shaw, Kathryn Howell, Rose Lernberg and me. Doll was now operating as our volunteer and going into the hills to trap only upon request from a homeowner. We also had two other trappers who helped out on an "as needed" basis—John LaMott and Dede Colette.

There was still money in the fund, so we could pay the telephone bill and veterinarian and boarding expenses. Every cent went directly towards firestorm animals. Any money that came in went to the Animal Care Clinic in San Pablo where we were now taking the pets we found. Drs. Evans and Lamp generously gave us a discount when we had to board animals with them while we attempted to find foster homes.

Every time we considered shutting down the operation, another flurry of activity would arise, and we would have numerous reports on more firestorm animals. One of the main reasons we continued the Hotline was the small group of "core" searchers. These fine people were still desperately looking for their cats. We had an open agreement to call them at any time of the day or night if we thought that a newly found pet might be theirs. The pain these people experienced was unimaginable. All they wanted was an answer—had their friend survived? They could deal with the possibility that the cat was dead, but just knowing that it might be out there and not in any sort of home was almost unbearable. Some of them told me that they would be willing to give up anything to get their companion back. It all seemed so unfair. On the one hand we had so many unclaimed fire zone pets, and on the other was this group of people who were willing to do anything to have their cat with them again.

The summer of 1992 continued to be busy. We were surprised and honored when we received word that the Hotline had received the prestigious "Give Life" Award from Living Free Sanctuary in Idyllwild, California. We found out that one of their board members lived in Contra Costa County, adjacent to Alameda County (where Berkeley and Oakland are located). He had heard about our rescue efforts and nominated our organization. The recipient of the individual award was the actress Doris Day for her continued work on behalf of animals. Our award was for the group category. We were thrilled and grateful for this recognition.

Around the Fourth of July, an independent rescuer had trapped a male cat near her home close to Lake Merritt. It was a real long shot that the cat might be a fire victim because Lake Merritt is in downtown Oakland, over five miles away from the fire zone, and across many busy streets. We came up with three possible matches and these people were called and asked to look at this buff colored cat with orange highlights and blue eyes. Stacey, the Hofmann's daughter, went to see the cat on the possibility that it might be the family's youngest cat, Max. When she saw him, she was sure that it was he and immediately telephoned her mother, Carol. As soon as she could get to him that day, Carol Hofmann knew for certain that it was the "baby" of the family. She immediately turned him upside down in her arms and Max snuggled into her and began purring, as Carol rocked him and cried. Three cats had been reunited with them over the nine months since the fire. The first, Cindy, had shown up at their property three days afterwards. Then Nellie was found in early May and now Max. Two of the family were still missing—Nadia and Natasha.

Immediately after Max's reunion, another cat was located and reunited. An orange tabby named Torger was less than seven blocks from his former home. He had been repeatedly sighted by a woman named Peggy who began to feed him and alerted us at the Hotline. We contacted numerous people who had cats that matched this one's description. Peggy was leaving on vacation, and took him to the vet's for boarding. Of the people we contacted, one family went to see the nine-year-old cat and recognized him as their Torger. To confirm that it was really their cat, the vet shined a light in Torger's eyes revealing an irregular pupil, and confirming the cat's identity. He had been so close by the whole time—or had he? Although he was in his former neighborhood, he might have been working his way back after fleeing in October. The media picked up the story and the Hotline received another flurry of telephone calls about potential fire survivor animals because of the new publicity.

These happy reunions were followed closely by another one in August of 1992. Although Misha, a seven-year-old gray and black tabby, had been evacuated from his home on Alvarado Road, he managed to escape the next day from an apartment in a neighborhood in Oakland, which is adjacent to the fire zone. He had jumped out of a second story window and Rita, his distraught owner, spent ten months searching the shelters, posting fliers and alerting neighbors. She made regular visits to the area, walking around and calling for the missing cat.

There had been two reported sightings of Misha during that time period, but he was so frightened that no one could catch him. Since her home had been spared, Rita thought that maybe Misha might try to get back to his old neighborhood, much of which was destroyed.

Encouraged by the knowledge that he was still out there, Rita decided to make one more attempt. She spent nearly fifty dollars on colorful, laminated posters and distributed them along the streets where the cat had escaped.

For days, nothing happened, and then on a Sunday in late August, a woman named Sharon, who lives close to the apartment, phoned Rita to say that the elusive Misha was devouring a can of tuna in her kitchen. Sharon had managed to lure the terrified cat into her home, and recognizing him from the picture on the posters, called Rita.

A quick trip and Misha was back with his family. His eyes looked a little sunken and his meow was not as strong as it once had been, but he looked fairly healthy. Rita attributed his survival to his hunting skills, but claimed that Misha would now be served only gourmet cat food. Rita's persistence had not been daunted by the advice of her neighbors who claimed that Misha was probably dead or so wild that he would not be the same if found. She refused to give up her search and it eventually paid off. As she hugged Misha for the first time since the fire, he lovingly nuzzled her neck.

The first anniversary of the fire was approaching. There were official acknowledgments of it in organized memorials, walks, and various gatherings among the neighborhood groups. Many of the people chose to remember it in their own way, some not at all. Having dealt with this rescue every day for all this time, I felt as if all of us at the Hotline were survivors from the firestorm as well. It had taken an emotional toll on us, but we just could not let the efforts end knowing that there was still the possibility of more reunions. I had worked on this project for a year now. My original estimate had been that it would only take two weeks, no longer than a month, to find all of the missing pets and reunite them with their owners. It was difficult to believe that a year had passed and there were still so many missing animals. Even more amazing was that the Hotline continued to get reports about firestorm animals that had been found. No report was dismissed as improbable. Each one was thoroughly researched in case it might be one of the pets that was not forgotten and was still so desperately missed.

Rose Lernberg decided to focus her efforts on other animal issues. Rose has been an animal rights advocate for a number of decades and spends a lot of time lobbying in the state capital. Knowing that she could be so much more effective there, and that this rescue was winding down, we sadly let her go. Her superb organizational skills and eye for the most minute detail contributed an immense amount to the Hotline. Rose delved into a lot of areas that might have been overlooked by someone else. Nothing slipped past her and the rescue effort owes a tremendous thank you to her for her dedication and thought-provoking analyses of situations.

Six more weeks passed. Patt suggested that we wrap it up at the end of the year, but Kathryn and I claimed that we were willing to devote a few hours a week to continuing the effort, since we now only met on Monday afternoons. The answering machine took messages during the rest of the week and we took turns checking it.

Any thought of closing down disappeared in mid-December. Kathryn had taken a report from a woman named Kelly who had seen a black and white cat in her neighborhood and had reported it to us. About a week later, she had spoken to her next door neighbors who casually mentioned to Kelly's horror that they had taken the stray cat to the pound.

Kathryn raced to the Berkeley City Pound the next day (not to be confused with Berkeley Humane Society) to get a photograph of the cat. There was only one other occupant of the cages that day, another black and white cat who made such a fuss, almost pleading for Kathryn to take her photgraph, too, that Kathryn did it just "on a whim."

Back at the Hotline, Patt and I pored over the two pictures of the similar cats. The one that Kelly had reported had no obvious matches, but the one that Kathryn had impulsively photographed strangely enough seemed to have four very distinct possibilities.

I telephoned the pound to enquire about the status of the two cats. Kelly's cat would be in for a week, but the other cat was due to be euthanized that afternoon at four o'clock, only ninety minutes away. I explained the situation to the staff person and asked if we could get a "stay of execution." The gentleman claimed that since the pound was mostly empty, they probably would not euthanize the cat today. Knowing how a bureaucracy can operate, I still insisted on getting a delay. It was granted. We called the four people whose cat it might be. One we ruled out over the phone because his did not have a white chin like this one. Three left. All were surprised to hear from us and were excited to think how wonderful it would be to have their cat home by Christmas after nearly fourteen months!

One actually had a picture attached to the report, but the young woman was holding the cat so that the chin was not visible. When I called her, Kristine Barrett-Davis said she could not remember how much white her cat had on its chin. She told me that the picture had been taken only the night before the fire and the roll of film was in her car as she escaped the next day.

The following day, there were three phone messages. Two stated that the cat was not theirs. The third was from Kristine Barrett-Davis, who was so excited she was crying. It was her cat, Disney! In order to have proof, Kristine asked the pound attendant to open the cat's mouth, and there was the undeniable proof—a zigzag black birthmark on the roof of her mouth.

The media had a field day with the story of the cat who was so close to death and was reunited just a week before Christmas. CNN picked it up and Associated Press did an interview for Christmas Day. *People* Magazine ran the story, as well. Ironically, Disney had been put into a "night drop" cage without any paperwork giving any indication of where she might have been all this time. Considering the season, it was speculated that an angel who was not carrying a pen might have been the one. It seemed as plausible a story as any other under the circumstances.

Without all the media attention that was lavished on Disney, Kathryn went to the pound on the final day of the other cat's allotted time and bailed her out. There was no possible way that this cat who had been so instrumental in Disney's rescue would be exterminated. It was the day before Christmas.

Following the extensive media coverage of Disney's story, the Hotline received numerous reports of other animals found that might possibly have been firestorm victims. Each of these, however distant, was followed up.

In late December 1992, we received a report about the Sheperd mix dog on Marlborough Terrace. It was not a construction worker's dog and it stayed away from all human contact, no matter how gentle or encouraging that contact might be. Some of the neighbors on the street had already rebuilt their homes and were beginning to try to pull the threads of their lives back together. A small canyon at the very end of the street had not burned when the wind shifted and took the fire in the opposite direction. The returning neighbors had thought that the dog had belonged at one of these homes, but did not recall ever having seen it before the fire. Yet it had lived along the street for the past thirteen months. Now that families were up in the fire zone at night, three different people reported it to the Hotline. The dog slept on one vacant lot and spent the day on another, silently observing all that went on around it. We had only one possible match for the Shepherd mix and when that party went by to see it, he knew that it was not his dog. Strangely, the dog seemed attached to the area and it was surmised that maybe because of the severe desolation the dog was confused and came from a parallel street farther down the hillside.

The weeks tumbled along and 1993 was here and established before anyone could get used to writing the new number. Reports continued to ebb and flow, but there were no reunions.

Winter fell away and the green grasses of spring carpeted the ashen hillsides. The residents of the fire zone were now seeing an emerging problem that no one had even considered: arson. In March, the nearly rebuilt home of a seventy-one-year-old widow burned down in the middle of a cold February night. It was clearly a case of arson. The widow had lost a child and her husband before the fire and still searched for her two cats, Thelma and Pauline, both eighteen years old at the time of the original fire in October 1991. Her dog had died only two months earlier, and now the rebuilt house had been burned down just a week before she was due to move back into it. Natural disasters are one thing, but an intentional fire of this sort that victimizes someone who has already suffered so much was reprehensible. Two more suspicious fires occurred before June, although no homes were damaged.

With hopes for reunions still high, in April 1993 the Hotline received a report about a cat that was being fed in the Broadway Terrace area. The woman, Bogna Laurence-Kot, had just heard about the Pet Rescue operation recently and told us of a stubby-tailed orange and white male that she had fed since the previous August. Her home had not burned, but she lived very close to the edge of the fire zone on Mountain Boulevard. Within ten minutes, we were in contact with Carol Martin whose cat, D.J., perfectly fit the description. By that evening, the family who had just returned to their rebuilt home, went to retrieve the cat, but ran into an unexpected problem. D.J. refused to come to them. He stayed at the back of the property where he was being fed and steadfastly rebuffed any actions taken to coax him to them. The Martins—Nick, Carol, Paul, thirteen, and his sister Jenny, eight years old—had really given up any hope of finding the family pet after they had found a cat claw on their property as they sifted through the rubble following the fire. At the time of the fire the Martins were hundreds of miles away attending a wedding. The ginger-colored Manx and Persian mix had been locked indoors and their next door neighbor came in to feed him. Before the fire was visible, the nieghbor had gone off with her family to a brunch in San Francisco, leaving D.J. to face the firestorm alone.

Now, here he was, but because of his extensive time out on his own, the docile cat who had lived indoors all of his life now decided to make his own rules.

Repeatedly, at six every morning and again every evening, the family would show up to feed D.J., hoping that this gesture would spark something in his memory. After talking with the family, I sensed that perhaps D.J. had not forgotten them after all. Perhaps he remembered just all too well who they were. From his standpoint, he may have blamed them for the fire and did not want to be placed in such a situation again. The weeks kept flipping by as the Martin's faithfully visited D.J. at his new residence. Carol Martin refused to give up. She is an extremely upbeat person. In speaking to her, you would never guess that she had lived through such an ordeal. Several other family members, including her elderly grandmother, also lost their own homes, yet Carol's spirit remained high. Her attitude was that D.J. has been found and they were joyous. It was only a matter of time before they would convince him to return home. Bogna graciously gave them an "open door" policy. They were welcome to come by whenever they chose to do so. Bogna was as excited about the reunion as the Martins and wanted to see D.J. return to the family who loved him so desperately. But as far as the Martins were concerned, if the elusive D.J. didn't want to come back with them, it was all right. He had survived and that was really all that mattered. He showed no real desires to leave Bogna's house. The Martin's continued their regular visits but they knew that a decision would have to be made soon.

In early June, Bogna's son called her from Hong Kong where he was on a business trip. Bogna related the unchanged status of the situation to him. He said "Leave it to me. When I get back, I will get that cat returned to the Martins."

True to his word, he managed to coax the cat into his mother's kitchen. It took a number of days of trying, but the cat finally came inside for the first time in twenty months.

Prepared for success, he grabbed D.J. and wrestled him into a carrier. Within fifteen minutes, D.J. was returned to his rightful home on Broadway Terrace.

D.J. did not show any signs of recognition. The house had been rebuilt almost exactly with the addition of a small breakfast nook, but aside from the floor plan, there was nothing familiar about the surroundings. Everything that had once been in the house was gone—ashes that had been hauled off long ago.

D.J. promptly found the laundry room and burrowed behind a pile of clothes. There he remained for almost forty-eight hours, finally emerging Sunday morning as if nothing had happened. The Martins, especially the children, were ecstatic about this complete turnaround in D.J.'s personality. He began to respond to the family and they began to resume the life that had been so abruptly truncated by the firestorm. D.J. was back home. Really back.

In July 1993, a tiny ad appeared in the classified section of the local newspaper, *The Montclarion*. It read: "William Bartley of Taurus Avenue—we found your cat, Katrina!" and it gave a telephone number to call.

Garnet Kympton, who had been Bartley's neighbor on Taurus Avenue, saw the ad and called Eric Gilliland, a friend who had lived with William before his death in 1989. Eric had only been able to rescue Katrina's two offspring as the fire hop-scotched along Taurus Avenue, sparing some houses and demolishing others. Eric's home was among those that the fire claimed in its last throes. Garnet was very surprised to see Katrina in her patio a few days after the fire, and immediately called Eric with the good news. By the time Eric reached the site, however, the cat was gone. Although he was relieved that Katrina had survived, he couldn't find her again, despite repeated attempts.

Taking the information from her collar, the family who found Katrina went in search of William Bartley, but to no avail. In desperation, they placed the ad.

Eric was stunned when Garnet called him and read the ad to him. Katrina had shown up after all this time! Even more amazing was where Katrina had appeared. She had somehow gotten to Alameda, California, which is an island in San Francisco Bay that runs parallel to the mainland and is linked to Oakland by a narrow bridge and a tunnel on its eastern side. It is over six miles from the fire zone across the entire city with its dangerous streets, freeways, and other hazards. By that evening, Eric and Katrina were happily reunited after twenty-one months apart.

The same week that D.J. finally moved back in with his family, we received a message on our machine about a dog, a long-haired Chihuahua, that had been found. He was in deplorable condition. He had apparently been living outside in Knowland Park where he had been found. He was malnourished, so covered with flea dirt that the coat color on his back could not be determined until he had been bathed, although he had a white head and feet. His nails had grown so long that they curved back under his paw pads, making him hobble. The woman fostering him, Marian Kendall, had volunteered to take him from an independent rescuer who had taken him out of the

Oakland Animal Shelter when his adoptive time had expired. Everyone was surprised that he had even been considered adoptable. It is a policy of many shelters to euthanize immediately when an animal is in extremely poor condition, such as this one was. When Monday came and we once again had access to the office, I looked at the reports. There was only one possible match for a long-haired Chihuahua. When I saw the address from which the dog had been lost, I mentally decreased his chances. Charing Cross Road had been one of the most devastated streets in the entire fire area. Eight people had died, including Officer John Grubensky as he tried to lead a group out. One man had been stopping in his van to pick up the stray dogs that were running down the hill, trying to get them out safely with him. All were found dead.

I called Teresa Berkeley who had filed the report about her dog, Timothy. It was one of the original reports that asked almost no information other than sex and breed and color, which was noted as "fawn." The report did not state if Timothy had been neutered or not. The dog who had been found had a testicular tumor.

Being very cautious not to get her excited, I told Teresa that this was such a minuscule possibility, but the dog had appeared to have been outside for such a long time it just might be Timothy. I told her the dog was at the veterinarian's being bathed and was having the tumor removed that afternoon. I gave Marian's telephone number to Teresa and encouraged her to go see the dog. Teresa was enthusiastic yet realistic. She did not hold out much hope of finding Timothy either. Her parents had barely escaped that day and called for him, but they were sure that he was inside. Their neighbor in the adjoining townhouse perished.

Marian called me at home to say that the Chihuahua was back and was recuperating well. I asked what color his coat had turned out to be.

"I would call it 'Fawn,' " she said.

It was exactly the term that Teresa had written in the tiny space on the form twenty months previously. At that second, my stomach twisted and I knew, just knew that we had a match.

Two hours later, a call from Marian and Teresa confirmed it.

Locked indoors, people and other animals dying all around him in the worst part of the blaze, Timothy had managed to survive. And now, because someone cared enough to make one phone call "just in case," the tiny dog was back with his family, almost two years later. At the Hotline, we were not only stunned to imagine that he survived the fire, but the intervening months as well. Such a tiny dog would be a perfect meal for one of the natural predators in the hills, such as hawks, coyotes, and raccoons.

Pehaps it was Timothy's size that saved him. Being so small, he could hide under rock outcroppings, in tiny burrows, or under just about anything. Larger dogs, while able to better protect themselves because of their size, would be more visible and would not have as many hiding spaces. They would also need larger amounts of food to survive. Half a discarded hot dog would be an entire meal for Timothy.

This pampered pet, who had lived his life indoors knowing only love and warmth and regular meals, was forced to survive outside through the cool, wet Northern California winter. But he did survive, in spite of all the hardships that befell him, and he was reunited with the family who loved him.

Part Four:
ANNIVERSARY

October 20, 1993

A week earlier, a scrawny, emaciated black and white cat wandered into the Piedmont Stables on Redwood Road. The owner of the stables, Irene, a concerned animal lover, took it to the veterinarian's and called the Hotline to let us know that she thought that it might be a fire survivor. Kathryn Howell went immediately to the vet's and photographed the cat and I placed the photo on the posterboard later that afternoon after we called all the people whose cat it might turn out to be. Two days later, on the second anniversary of the fire, Noreen Cardinale positively identified the cat as her Sammy. She had lived in Hiller Highlands with Bob Wagoner, whom she always called "Bobby." He was diagnosed with cancer within a month after the fire, and died on October 3, 1993. Oddly, when the good Samaritan took the cat to the vet's, she had to pick out a name for it for filing and identification purposes. She chose "Bobby." Noreen believes there was a definite connection between Bobby's passing and Sammy's return, and feels that Bobby sent the cat back to her to help ease her grief. So much had been taken away from her, but now some of her former life had been returned.

On Marlborough Terrace, the homes continued to be rebuilt. The German Sherpherd mix sat throughout the seasons, carefully observing the human movements as the huge trucks lumbered up the narrow street disgorging the materials that would be transformed into homes once more. It gratefully but warily accepted remnants of the workmen's lunches and the bowls of food and water left out for it by the concerned neighbors. However, no amount of searching could lead to any clues about the dog's past.

One day in midsummer, the dog joyfully and quite uncharacteristically greeted a houseguest of one of the survivors, an older woman with white hair. It was the first human contact that the dog allowed itself to have in almost two years. That gave us a clue. Perhaps its owner was an older woman. When it was researched, it turned out that a sixty-one-year old woman with white hair had died in the fire and had lived on a parallel street, but it turned out that this woman had never had a dog such as this one.

Steven and Sybil Maguire could see the dog sitting, watching on the hillside opposite their home, and consistently left food out for it. Eventually they were able to coax it to them and to pet it. After a few weeks, the dog took up residence on their deck. Not really wanting a dog, the couple nevertheless fell in love with her. Within two weeks, the dog had adopted them and proved to be a highly trained, extremely well-behaved animal. Her change was sudden and dramatic. The dog who had always cowered with her tail between her legs now gleefully wags it.

One survivor had bonded with the others, and the Maguires formally adopted the dog whom they now call

"Q.T." She is doted upon and given the love and companionship that she denied herself all those lonesome months on the hillside. It was only appropriate that those who have lost such a tremendous amount can find happiness with one another and help to ease the burden of resuming their lives together.

At the time of this writing, two years have passed since the firestorm. The fire has become one of the defining moments of our lives here in the Bay Area, one of those times where you will remember where you were and what you were doing. Disaster hovers over us, yet we continue to live with the dangers, knowing that at any second an earthquake or fire might take away all that is precious to us, yet most of us choose to remain here. It is our home and we will face whatever nature intends for us. It is a trade off, actually. We live with the fear so that we may enjoy the tremendous benefits of this region.

Homes are rising again on the hillsides of Oakland and Berkeley. Very few of those who lost homes have chosen not to rebuild. A number of people lost their homes in the 1970 fire, yet returned to the area and rebuilt again. Almost twenty-five percent of the homes are in the process of rebuilding, some having been finished and occupied for a year now. It will be a long time before the rebuilding and the reforestation is complete, but it will occur. Slowly life resumes its beat on the barren hillsides. Green leaves appear on charred stumps, salamanders slither under the crumbling foundations on empty lots.Life is there, and although it seems to have the pace of a snail at times, it will triumph where there was only the pulverizing destruction of an uncontrollable firestorm two short years earlier.

The Firestorm Pet Hotline continues in operation to this day. What began as a possible six-week venture has turned into a two-year odyssey. Being the first organized rescue of domestic pets on this large scale, we had no idea how long it might take.

We are dedicated to finding as many of the surviving animals as possible. Each phone call just might be the one that reunites some grieving person with their beloved companion, and we want to make certain that we are there to get that call, and be that link to the happiness of a reunion. There were 294 cats and 101 dogs that were reunited in the two years following the fire. How we wish we could have found them all.

Afterword

S hortly after this book was completed, firestorms devastated southern California, erupting in Laguna Beach and Sierra Madre. A few days later, another, larger firestorm swept through Laurel Canyon and hours later reached the Pacific Ocean at Malibu. Among the dead was a man who was attempting to rescue his cat. That cat did survive, although it was profoundly injured. An organized animal rescue effort was underway in the first hours following the fire. However, this situation was notably different from the conditions described in this book. Many residents had advance warning and the majority of animals in the threatened areas were safely evacuated.

Less than ninety days afterwards, on January 17, 1994, a killer earthquake with a magnitude of 6.6, shattered the Los Angeles area. Again, a highly organized animal rescue effort was on the scene within the first few hours, minimizing the disastrous effects to the local pets.

Firestorms also erupted around Sydney, Australia. Erratic wind shifts caused extensive destruction when areas thought to be safe suddenly were in the firestorm's path. The animal populations suffered tremendous losses, including a colony of koalas and a mob of kangaroos.

Nowhere in the world is one completely safe from disaster, but we can minimize the impact these disasters have on our animals if we take precautions. A pre-arranged disaster plan is now a necessary fact of life (see the disaster guide on page 168). Of equal importance is the devotion and determination of people who come together and offer aid to the most vulnerable—human and animal alike. Without the generosity of the volunteers at the Hotline and throughout the pet rescue operation, most of the displaced creatures would never have found their families again.

EPILOGUE

Pumpkin continues to do well. She has had two major cosmetic surgeries, but has healed as best she can. Diana and her family have moved back into their rebuilt home. Their other cat, Samantha, has resumed a normal existence.

Margaret Power, who fled to safety in the police car with her neighbor, Juanita Simpson, was one of the first people to move back into her rebuilt home. Her cat, Mittens, has not been found.

Juanita Simpson's two cats, Cassey and Trent, both returned to their home site, and all are living in their rebuilt house. Melvin, who narrowly escaped with her in the police car, recently celebrated his twenty-first birthday.

Norma Armon's children gave her a Birman kitten that had been born on the day of the fire as a gift for Christmas 1991. She named it Vishnu, after the Hindu goddess of fire. Norma is rebuilding and frequently visits Charmian's grave.

Yves and Dawn Mottier were reunited with four of their seven cats, two of whom have since died of natural causes.

Babe's body was found in the ruins of his home.

Mamalucci continues to be himself.

The Dobson family has only Tao left. MaMa escaped from a temporary home in which they were living and has not been found. Mimi and Skids were killed by automobiles at another temporary home in Oakland.

Disney escaped from her rebuilt home on Alvarado Road in June 1993, when a contractor left the door open. She has not been seen since. The cat who was so instrumental in helping to reunite Disney is thriving in her new home.

Chad continues to live in his foster home until Jay Stewart has finished rebuilding. He spends the weekends with Jay. The apartment management still tolerates the situation.

Dudley and Stan Smith have tried to resume their normal lives. Dudley refuses to let Stan out of his sight and accompanies him to the office.

Bud, Princess, Nikki, Timothy, Max (Hofmann), Max (Smith), D.J., Blackie, Zeb, Gus, and C.T. are adjusted and back to normal routines. Natasha and Nadia Hofmann have not been found.

Q.T. has become an adored member of the Maguire family and continues to do well.

The fire marshall of the State of California personally inspected Don Proia and GeorgeAnn Hemingway-Proia's home, but could not explain why it alone was spared. Casey and Ginger are inseparable.

Gallagher and Ethel King happily moved into their rebuilt townhouse in Hiller Highlands in the spring of 1993. Because of a rodent infestation caused by all of the rebuilding, many neighbors left out poison and Gallagher became critically ill. Ethel refused to euthanize him and he later fully recovered.

Dave Stewart, who was rescued shortly after the fire, disappeared a month later and has not yet been found.

The three orphan kittens found in the crevice were placed in foster care until they were eight weeks old and nicknamed Fire, Wind, and Storm. All three were adopted by families who lost their homes that day.

Mr. Fox is the only animal fire survivor who actually gave me a direct interview. He sat with his two paws on my knee and intently watched my face. Esther and Fritze merely supplied the words for him.

A Disaster Guide for Pet Owners

Before the disaster:

1. **Take photos of your pets and have copies else-where**—in a safe deposit box, or with an out-of-area friend or relative. These photos can be invaluable in helping you to remember the pet's specific traits and to help the rescue personnel identify the pet. Be sure to write the name and date on the reverse of each photograph.

2. **Have a phone number where you can be reached for an extended period of time.** Do not give rescue personnel the number of a hotel or shelter, which will be invalid in only a few days.

3. **Identify your pet.** Collar and tag (with up-to-date information, including rabies vaccinations), micro-chip, tattoo, etc. There are many ways to identify your animal.

4. **Keep carriers and leashes accessible.** Familiar-ize your pet with the carrier beforehand, so the confine-ment will not be frightening. Bird cages may be difficult to handle, so have a smaller one available to use for trans-portation. Keep boxes accessible if you have exotic pets, such as reptiles or ducks.

5. Have a pre-arranged disaster plan. Write it out in large, readable letters that could be seen by a flashlight beam if necessary. Keep it with the pet carrier or leash. It is recommended that you have three plans developed: one for a five-minute (or less) evacuation, a fifteen-minute plan, and a forty-five minute plan. Once the animals are secure, you can read off your list and gather the things that you have determined you should take. List the objects *and* their locations. Keep this or another resource guide with your disaster material.

During the disaster:

The duration of this critical period will vary greatly. A hurricane might last for a significant amount of time, whereas an earthquake is over in less than a minute. There might be ample warning for some, none at all for others. Sometimes you will not be able to locate your pets, so be aware of favorite hiding places

1. Do not leave your animals behind if it is necessary to evacuate. If you are given warning, capture your pets as soon as possible and confine them. Be prepared to leave on a moment's notice. Although it may not look as if your home might be harmed, you may get a rude awakening. Aftershocks, wind shifts, etc., may account for the loss of your property.

2. Do not believe the authorities or the media. Major mistakes may have been made in calculations, and these people are only human, too. This is a disaster, and everyone is affected. The police and fire emergency services might be overwhelmed in an incredibly short time, so depend only on yourself. This is the point where you might have to take matters into your own hands. Do not assume that it will all be brought under control just because you called 9-1-1.

3. **If you have located your animal, keep all outside doors and windows closed until you leave with your pet**. While you are racing around, opening and closing doors, your pet will take the first available chance to flee.

4. **If forced to evacuate without your pet, leave doors and windows open so it can flee**. The pet may have already evacuated without you, but it might be hiding in your house, so leave the house open.

If you have found your pet and are absolutely unable to transport it, set it free. You will at least be giving the animal a chance to survive. If you just cannot carry that cage of finches, let them go.

After the disaster:

1. Although easier said than done, **try to remain calm**. It will be better for you and your pet if one of you is not hysterical. Read your disaster plan. In moments such as these, it is very easy to overlook the obvious.

2. If you have lost a pet, begin searching immediately. Check all of the animal shelters on a regular basis.

Remember that no one knows your pet the way you do, so you must do the searching.

3. Find out if there is an organized pet rescue. Keep in mind that the pet's appearance may have changed. File a report as soon as possible and get those photos of your pet to the rescue service.

4. Do not assume anything, especially that your pet did not survive. You might be surprised. Survival is one of the strongest of any animal's instincts.

5. Visit your property frequently. Many animals are territorial and will return if possible. Leave out food and water and an unwashed article of your clothing. Build a shelter if the weather is bad.

6. Above all else, **DO NOT GIVE UP!** Months or even years might elapse before a pet is found. Keep up the search. Persistence pays off!

A special note to Californians: Our usual disasters, earthquakes and fires, strike with deadly, rapid force. Although we might have some warning of an approaching fire, earthquakes hit us suddenly. We do not have the luxury of advance warning, so we must be prepared to deal with disaster at all times. We must learn from the recent, unfortunate experiences of our neighbors and take all precautions necessary to ensure the survival and well-being of our families and our pets.